# REFORMATION, EXPLORATION, AND EMPIRE

Volume 9

SHAH ABBAS THE GREAT–TEXTILES

an imprint of

www.scholastic.com/librarypublishing

Published by Grolier,
an imprint of Scholastic Library Publishing,
Sherman Turnpike
Danbury, Connecticut 06816

Set ISBN 0-7172-6071-2
Volume 9 ISBN 0-7172-6080-1

Library of Congress Cataloging-in-Publication Data

Reformation, exploration, and empire.
    p. cm.
    Contents: Vol. 1. Academies–Catherine de Médicis —
v. 2. Catholic church–daily life — v. 3. Decorative arts–
fortifications — v. 4. France–inventions and inventors —
v. 5. Ireland–manufacturing — v. 6. Maps and
mapmaking–Orthodox church — v. 7. Ottoman Empire–
printing — v. 8. Privacy and luxury–sculpture — v. 9.
Servants–textiles — v. 10. Thirteen Colonies–Zwingli.
    Includes bibliographical references and index.
    ISBN 0-7172-6071-2 (set : alk. paper) — ISBN 0-7172-
6072-0 (v. 1 : alk. paper) — ISBN 0-7172-6073-9 (v. 2 :
alk. paper) — ISBN 0-7172-6074-7 (v. 3 : alk. paper) —
ISBN 0-7172-6075-5 (v. 4 : alk. paper) — ISBN 0-7172-
6076-3 (v. 5 : alk. paper) — ISBN 0-7172-6077-1 (v. 6 :
alk. paper) — ISBN 0-7172-6078-X (v. 7 : alk. paper) —
ISBN 0-7172-6079-8 (v. 8 : alk.paper) — ISBN 0-7172-
6080-1 (v. 9 : alk. paper) — ISBN 0-7172-6081-X (v. 10 :
alk. paper)
    1. History, Modern—16th century—Encyclopedias,
Juvenile. 2. History, Modern—17th century—
Encyclopedias, Juvenile. 3 Renaissance—Encyclopedias,
Juvenile. 4 Civilization, Modern—17th century—
Encyclopedias, Juvenile. 5 Reformation—Encyclopedias,
Juvenile. I. Grolier (Firm)

    D228.R46 2005
    909'.5'03—dc22                          2004063255

For information address the publisher:
Grolier, Sherman Turnpike,
Danbury, Connecticut 06816

### FOR THE BROWN REFERENCE GROUP

Project Editor:               Emily Hill
Deputy Editor:                Tom Webber
Text Editors:                 Rachel Bean
                              Jane Edmonds
Picture Researcher:           Susy Forbes
Maps:                         Darren Awuah
Design Manager:               Lynne Ross
Design:                       Q2A Solutions
Production Director:          Alastair Gourlay
Editorial Director:           Lindsey Lowe
Senior Managing Editor:       Tim Cooke
Consultant:                   Prof. James M. Murray
                              University of Cincinnati

Printed and bound in Singapore

# ABOUT THIS SET

This is one of a set of 10 books about the key period of western history from around 1500 to around 1700. The defining event of the age was the Reformation, the attempt to reform the Catholic church that resulted in a permanent split in western Christianity. The period was also marked by the European exploration and colonization of new lands, profound political change, and dynamic cultural achievement.

The roots of the Reformation lay in a tradition of protest against worldliness and corruption in the Catholic church. In 1517 the German Augustinian monk Martin Luther produced a list of criticisms of Catholicism and sparked a protest movement that came to be known as Protestantism. The reformers broke away from Catholicism and established new Protestant churches. In response the Catholic church launched the Counter Reformation, its own program of internal reforms.

Religious change had a profound political influence as Protestantism was adopted by various rulers to whom it offered a useful way to undermine Europe's existing power structures. The period was one of intolerance, persecution, and almost continuous warfare. Meanwhile new approaches to religion combined with the spread of printing and increased literacy to produce a knowledge revolution in which new ideas flourished about science, art, and humanity's place in the universe.

Changes in Europe had a lasting effect on events elsewhere. Spanish conquistadors overthrew vast empires in the Americas, while Catholic missionaries spread Christianity in Africa, the Americas, and Asia. Gradually lands in the east and the west were penetrated and colonized by Europeans. These and other important changes, such as the development of international trade, great cultural achievements, and the spirit of learning, are explored in detail in each volume.

While focusing mainly on Europe, the set also looks at important developments across Africa, Asia, and the Americas. Each entry ends with a list of cross references to related entries so that you can follow up particular topics. Contemporary illustrations give a fuller picture of life during the Reformation. Each volume contains a glossary, a "Further Reading" list that includes websites, a timeline, and an index covering the whole set.

# Contents

## Volume 9

# SHAH ABBAS THE GREAT

**The great Safavid ruler Shah Abbas I (ruled 1588–1629) controlled vast territories in Persia (now Iran) and reinforced Safavid power by expelling Ottomans and Uzbeks from his lands. He made Esfahan the capital of the Safavid Empire and developed Persian trade and arts to a high level.**

The Safavid Empire appeared to be in terminal decline by the 1580s. Under the rule of Abbas's father, Shah Mohammad (ruled 1577–1588), the empire was torn apart by civil war and invaded by the Uzbeks in the east and the Ottomans in the west. Many of the Qizilbash—powerful Turkic chiefs whose support had helped the Safavids maintain their authority—lost faith in Mohammad as a spiritual leader. They assasinated his eldest son to make way for their own candidate.

Mohammad's third son, Abbas, was sent to safety in Khorasan, a region in northeastern Persia. Abbas decided to overthrow his father and restore strong Safavid rule. In 1586 he headed an army of loyal tribesmen and marched on the capital city, Kazvin. His revolt was successful, and in 1588 Abbas became shah (sovereign).

## CONSOLIDATING POWER

Abbas immediately smashed the power of the Qizilbash, confiscating their lands and instituting new tribal confederacies (leagues). Abbas then moved against rebellious tribes: He ordered a general massacre of the population of the Black Sea province of Gilan in 1592 to serve as a warning to other nomadic tribes in the region.

Having secured his kingdom from internal dissent, in 1598 Abbas moved his capital to Esfahan in the protected heart of his realm. There he ordered the construction of palaces, parks, gardens, mosques, religious schools, and factories, making it the most beautiful city in West Asia. Esfahan became the focus for a great flowering of Persian art and literature.

## ESTABLISHING A LOYAL ARMY

To maintain his authority, protect his empire, and reduce his dependence on the Qizilbash military units, Abbas

*Shah Abbas attacks an Uzbek soldier in this wall painting made around 1600 to decorate the imperial palace in Esfahan. The painting celebrates one of Abbas's victories over the Uzbeks in the late 1590s.*

created a standing (permanent) army of his own. To make sure that its soldiers remained loyal, Abbas recruited former Christian prisoners-of-war who had converted to Islam. Abbas appointed two English adventurers, Anthony and Robert Sherley, to introduce the latest European military technology into his army, including muskets, cannons, and modern battlefield tactics.

Abbas also wanted more diplomatic contacts with Europe. However, the Ottoman Empire blocked trade routes and lines of communication to the west of Persia. Abbas dispatched Anthony Sherley to Europe as an ambassador to secure European support for a war against the Ottomans.

## MILITARY CAMPAIGNS

Abbas's armies had been engaged in a long war against the Uzbeks in the east. When the Uzbek khan (ruler) died in 1598, Abbas took advantage of the ensuing civil war to reconquer Herat (in present-day Afghanistan) and to stabilize the eastern frontier of his empire. To the south he reestablished the border with Mogul India at Kandahar, although skirmishes in the region continued throughout his reign.

Finally Abbas turned to the Persian lands that had been conquered by the Ottomans. With his new army he defeated a combined Turkish–Mongol army and retook Tabriz and most of Azerbaijan. The war continued as Persia fought to reclaim Iraq, capturing Baghdad in 1623. By 1629 Abbas had restored the empire to its borders under the first Safavid shah, Esmail I (ruled 1501–1524).

## TRADE WITH EUROPE

Shah Abbas granted the English East India Company the right to trade in Esfahan and at Jask, on the Persian Gulf. In 1622 the company's ships

helped Abbas dislodge the Portuguese from Hormuz, the key stronghold on the Persian Gulf. Abbas established a new trading port at Bandar Abbas, where English cloth was traded for Persian silk. Trade drew Abbas closer to Europe: The Persians were both intermediaries in the trade between Europe and India and allies against the Ottomans. Abbas developed overland trade in his empire, building new roads and bridges and importing skilled merchants from Armenia. He also centralized the carpet-weaving industry, insisting on high standards that made Persian carpets world famous.

The last years of Shah Abbas's reign were marred by his paranoid fear of rebellion from within his own family. He confined his sons to the harem, then he had his eldest son killed and his two remaining sons blinded to make them unfit to rule. After Abbas died in 1628, Persia's fortunes declined.

*This photograph shows part of the Royal Mosque in Esfahan. Built between 1612 and 1637 on the orders of Shah Abbas, the mosque is one of the many buildings with which he beautified his new capital city.*

SEE ALSO

• Esfahan
• Islam
• Merchants
• Ottoman Empire
• Persia
• Persian–Ottoman wars

# SHAH JAHAN

The fifth Mogul emperor of India, Shah Jahan (ruled 1628–1658), was not only a man of action but also a sensitive patron of culture. His reign witnessed a great flowering of Mogul art and architecture; he built the Taj Mahal, one of world's most beautiful buildings.

Born in 1592, with the name Khurram, the future Shah Jahan was one of the younger sons of the Mogul Emperor Jahangir. He raised an unsuccessful rebellion against his father in 1622 but was subsequently pardoned. In 1628 he finally succeeded his father and secured his position by murdering most of his male relatives. He gave himself the title Shah Jahan ("king of the world") and embarked on a series of campaigns in which he conquered most of the Deccan region in central India. He also destroyed both Hindu temples and Christian churches.

Alongside his capacity for violence Shah Jahan had a profound love of beauty, especially in the sphere of architecture. He adorned his new capital of Delhi with an impressive array of buildings, including the Great Mosque and the Red Fort, which was not only a luxurious palace but also the center of the imperial government.

*Shah Jahan sits surrounded by courtiers in this 18th-century miniature. The Taj Mahal is in the background. It is said that after being imprisoned in a fort in Agra in 1658 by his son, Aurangzeb, Shah Jahan spent his days gazing with melancholy at the Taj Mahal, his beloved wife's beautiful tomb.*

In 1657 Shah Jahan fell seriously ill, and his four sons then fought among themselves to succeed him. The victorious Aurangzeb imprisoned him in a fort in Agra, where he died in 1666.

## THE TAJ MAHAL

The Taj Mahal is the world's most famous mausoleum. It was built overlooking the Jumna River at Agra by Shah Jahan in memory of his wife Mumtaz Mahal, who died in childbirth in June 1631. No expense was spared in creating the domed building and its ornamental gardens. Up to 20,000 workers were employed for more than 20 years, creating the Taj out of creamy white marble and embellishing it with precious gemstones, such as malachite and lapis lazuli. Beneath the dome were placed the inlaid marble tombs of Mumtaz and Shah Jahan, united in death as they had been united in life.

SEE ALSO
• Akbar
• Architecture
• Esfahan
• India
• Islam
• Persia
• Persian–Ottoman wars

# SHAKESPEARE, WILLIAM

Shakespeare (about 1564–1616) is widely acknowledged as the greatest English dramatist and poet. He was also an actor in the most successful acting troupe of his time. During his career he wrote 37 plays, 5 narrative poems, and a sequence of 154 sonnets.

William Shakespeare was born in Stratford-on-Avon traditionally on April 23, 1564. Little is known about his life. In 1582 he married Anne Hathaway. They had three children: Susanna and twins christened Hamnet and Judith.

About four years after his marriage Shakespeare was charged with killing a deer. He gave up his job in Stratford—he was probably a schoolmaster—and moved to London, where he met Lord Southampton, who became his patron. By 1592 Shakespeare had established himself as an actor with the Lord Chamberlain's Company and was gaining a reputation as a poet and playwright. His first published work was *Venus and Adonis* (1593), a narrative poem.

*This is an engraving of a portrait of Shakespeare, which was probably by the English actor and painter Richard Burbage (about 1567–1619), with whom Shakespeare performed many of his own plays.*

## SHAKESPEARE'S WORKS

The chronology of Shakespeare's plays is disputed, but among the earliest were *Titus Andronicus* (1593–1594) and *Henry VI Parts I and II* (1597–1598), which may have been updates of older works, now lost, by other playwrights. The first play in which Shakespeare shows his genius is generally agreed to be *Love's Labours Lost* (about 1594).

By 1597 Shakespeare had earned enough money to buy the second-largest house in Stratford. His success to this point was founded principally on history plays and comedies such as *The Merry Wives of Windsor* (1600). From 1599 his dramatic works were first performed at the Globe, a newly built theater that he partly owned.

After 1601 Shakespeare wrote more tragedies. His greatest works in this genre are *Hamlet* and *Othello* (both 1604) and *King Lear* and *Macbeth* (1606). His last play, *The Tempest* (1611–1612), is a romantic drama.

By 1610 Shakespeare had left the theater and returned to Stratford, where he died on April 23, 1616.

SEE ALSO

- Drama
- Elizabeth I
- England
- Language
- Poetry
- Tudor family

# SHIPS

**The period from the late 15th century to the end of the 18th century is often called the age of exploration. Developments in marine technology made global travel possible. Ships carried sailors, civilians, and goods across oceans to the most distant corners of the world.**

Until the 15th century most sea travel was along coastlines or within local seas. The principal European sailing vessel of the early 1400s was the galley, the design of which dated from ancient Greece.

Although the galley had masts and sails—some of the largest English and Spanish vessels carried up to four masts—it still relied on ranks of oars projecting from the hull to provide its main source of propulsion and maneuverability. Above the deck line of the vessel there were two "castles," large built-up structures at the front and back of the boat, known respectively as the forecastle and the aftcastle.

Castles provided a number of useful facilities, such as extra storage space, living quarters for the crew, and gun platforms. However, they made vessels top-heavy, increasing the danger of rolling over in heavy weather; because they caught the wind, they also affected a vessel's steering.

### OCEAN-GOING SHIPS

Oar power was fine for short- or medium-range journeys, but in the 15th century European nations increasingly needed ocean-going vessels as they began to make long-distance voyages of exploration. The Portuguese developed a sturdy ship called a caravel to make voyages in the Atlantic down the coast of Africa. The seaworthiness of the caravel made it a popular vessel

for exploration, and it was used by mariners such as Vasco da Gama (about 1460–1524), Christopher Columbus (1451–1506), and John Cabot (about 1450–1499) to make epic voyages of discovery in the east and west.

The caravel was developed from Atlantic and Mediterranean fishing boats. The version made for long-distance travel typically had three masts of sail, including a lateen sail on the rear mast. This triangular sail made the

*The English galleon* Resolution *steers a course through a rough sea in this painting by the famous 17th-century Dutch marine artist Willem van de Velde II.*

*This colored print shows the shipyard and warehouses at the headquarters of the Dutch East India Company in Amsterdam. The company, founded in 1602, required many ships for its trade with Asia. By 1670 the Netherlands had more ships than England, France, Portugal, and Spain put together.*

caravel very maneuverable and capable of sailing into the wind. Caravels had a length-to-breadth (width) ratio of about 5:1 and a weight of around 100 tons (102 tonnes), and handled well in rough seas. However, they had limited space for storing cargo. During the 16th century Portugal, Spain, France, the Netherlands, and later England established trading colonies in the Americas, around the African coastline, and as far east as China.

These far-flung outposts required improved maritime (sea-going) vessels if they were to be efficiently maintained and protected, and their full trade potential was to be realized. Although caravels were used into the 1600s, they were superseded by carracks.

### THE CARRACK

The carrack was a type of ship that originated in the Mediterranean region and was introduced into northern European fleets. Carracks were usually large three-masted vessels suited to ocean travel. As their design was modified, carracks came to feature much larger sails, with a corresponding increase in the size of the vessel, storage capacity, and defensive armament. The forecastles and

aftcastles also underwent substantial increases in size, despite continuing problems of instability.

While the Portuguese and Spanish were great carrack builders, it was the English who came to construct some of the most impressive examples. The 16th century was the beginning of the Royal Navy's rise to supremacy, as underlined by such majestic carracks as the *Henry Grâce à Dieu* (1514) and the *Mary Rose* (1510). The *Mary Rose* weighed 600 tons (610 tonnes), although rebuilding in the 1530s increased the ship's weight by a further 100 tons (102 tonnes). The vessel was heavily armed and became the second most powerful ship in the English fleet after the 1,500-ton (1524-tonne) *Henry Grâce à Dieu*. The *Mary Rose* sank on July 19, 1545, when strong winds turned the ship over and sent it to the bottom of the sea.

The fate of the *Mary Rose* demonstrates the vulnerability of the carrack in strong winds. Because of its large castles it was also inefficient when sailing into the wind—the castles broke the flow of wind to the sails. By the mid-16th century, however, there was an important new development in ship design: the galleon.

### THE GALLEON

The galleon was a heavily armed vessel, typically with three masts. Galleons were used as armed merchant (trade) vessels for ocean voyages or as warships. At first galleons differed from carracks mainly in their dimensions, having a greater length-to-width ratio to make the ship more maneuverable, faster, and more seaworthy. The forecastle was moved farther back from the ship's front, and a bowsprit sail was placed in front of it to break the wind before it hit the forecastle—on the carrack the bowsprit projected forward from the forecastle itself.

*An armed merchant ship and other vessels lie anchored in port in this 17th-century Dutch painting. The artist, Cornelis Claesz van Wieringen (about 1580–1633), was a sailor before he became a painter.*

In around 1574 English galleons improved. Ships such as the 500-ton (508-tonne) *Revenge* had lower castles; distinct castles steadily disappeared from the galleon as time went on. They also had better rigging and more slender dimensions, which made them excellent for long voyages and for moving quickly in combat. In addition new galleons had flatter sails, which improved the ships' handling in rough weather. Galleries were added to many galleons. These open balconies projected from the ship to increase deck space; later they were covered to provide officers' quarters.

Galleons remained the most important type of European sailing ship for more than 100 years. Yet the amount of weaponry they carried often restricted the amount of nonmilitary cargo that they could transport. During the 1500s the Dutch created the *fluyt*, which was purely a merchant vessel. The *fluyt* was ingenious in that it had a

## SCURVY

In the 16th century mariners faced a host of diseases because of poor diet and unsanitary living conditions. Surgeons often traveled on board ships and were able to perform operations such as amputation and give sailors basic medicines. But for those who fell seriously ill at sea, there was little the physician could do since understanding of diseases was so limited.

From 1500 the main killer at sea was scurvy. Caused by vitamin deficiencies, especially of Vitamin C—found in citrus fruits such as oranges and lemons—scurvy frequently struck sailors on long voyages. Their diet lacked fresh fruit and vegetables, since it consisted largely of dried foods such as biscuits, salted meats, and fish caught while at sea. On the Portuguese explorer Vasco da Gama's voyage to India in 1497–1499, 60 percent of the crew died from the disease. The explorer Ferdinand Magellan lost 80 percent of his men to scurvy while crossing the Pacific Ocean.

Symptoms of scurvy were very unpleasant—sufferers felt weak and depressed, they had bleeding and swollen gums, their teeth fell out, their skin erupted in boils and black-and-blue marks appeared, their joints were stiff and sore, and it became increasingly difficult to breathe. In the later stages of the disease they fell into a coma and died within days. Scurvy claimed the lives of thousands of sailors throughout the 16th and 17th centuries. It was not until 1753 that the Scottish surgeon James Lind (1716–1794) linked the illness with a vitamin deficiency and showed that drinking the juice of citrus fruits prevents scurvy.

# PUNISHMENT AT SEA

Ships' captains maintained very strict discipline among the crew while at sea and administered a variety of punishments for crimes, some of which were very harsh. A sailor caught stealing might be forced to "run the gauntlet," in which he had to pass between two rows of his ship-mates who rained down blows on him with clubs or their fists. On some ships punishment for stealing was to be tarred and feathered—the offender was covered with hot tar, which often caused considerable burns, and then sprinkled with bird feathers. For using a knife during a fight, a sailor might have his knife-hand cut off. For murder a typical 16th-century English naval punishment was to tie the killer to the body of his victim and then throw them both overboard.

Another punishment for serious crimes, such as murder and mutiny, was "keel-haul-ing." The offender was tied to a long rope, thrown over the side, and dragged underneath the ship from one side to the other. The hull was usually encrusted with rough barnacles, so if the victim did not drown, he would often be sliced open on the barnacles—in tropical waters his blood might also attract shark attacks. Most people who were keel-hauled died from the punishment.

*Mutinous sailors are thrown overboard for keel-hauling in this 16th-century illustration.*

wide body near the waterline—and so was very stable and could carry lots of cargo—but narrowed sharply up toward the deck. A narrow deck meant that fewer sailors were needed, thereby reducing the amount of provisions required and so increasing the cargo space. The *fluyt* was such a success that the Netherlands became the leading merchant-shipping nation of the 1600s.

The refinement of sailing ships during the age of exploration was an important development in the history of transportation. Although slow—a galleon could sail at about 10mph (16km/h) with a good wind—and often thrown off course by poor navigation, carracks and galleons enabled the European nations to lay the foundations of overseas empires.

**SEE ALSO**

- Anglo-Dutch Naval Wars
- Colonization
- Exploration
- Maps and mapmaking
- Naval power
- Navigation
- Pirates and brigands

# SICKNESS AND DISEASE

**Death was an everyday reality for all people, whether rich or poor, in the 16th and 17th centuries. Lack of medical knowledge, particularly with regard to how disease spread and how to treat it, meant that epidemics regularly decimated populations across Europe and the rest of the world.**

The most feared disease in 1500 was the bubonic plague—70 to 100 percent of those infected died. It may have been responsible for the deaths of up to a third of Europe's population in the Black Death between 1348 and 1351. An epidemic on such a huge scale did not occur again, but there were many major outbreaks in the 16th and 17th centuries. In London, for example, there were five outbreaks of plague between 1563 and 1603, in which 30,000 died. In the Great Plague of 1664–1665 more than 70,000 died—15 percent of the city's population.

The disease was spread by black rats infested with fleas that carried the infection. It moved from country to country on rat-ridden ships. The first signs of infection included shivering, vomiting, and pain in the back and limbs, followed by the appearance of buboes (painful swellings) in the groin and armpits. A common treatment was to be bled, although this was useless. The poor made do with remedies such as drinking their own urine. Nothing prevented a painful death.

The disease was best avoided by fleeing to the countryside, a course of action taken by wealthy townspeople. Those who were left behind had to endure being locked in their homes if any member of their family contracted the disease. By 1700 plague epidemics had lessened dramatically, although there continued to be isolated outbreaks into the 20th century.

## SYPHILIS

While the wealthy could escape the plague, they were as likely as everyone else to be the victims of two other major infectious diseases: syphilis and smallpox. It was once thought that

*The figure of death confronts a young woman in this 17th-century painting. At a time when there were no effective cures for a large number of killer diseases, many people died early in life.*

*Plague victims are cared for in Perugia, Italy, in this illustration from a 16th-century manuscript. There was little that could be done to relieve the suffering of plague victims. None of the suggested remedies, which ranged from herbs to fantastical concoctions such as smoked horses' testicles, could eradicate the buboes and fever that usually resulted in death.*

syphilis was brought by Christopher Columbus's crew from the Americas to Europe. However, it is more likely that it evolved from a nonfatal disease called yaws. Syphilis caused open ulcers and abscesses over the entire body, and often killed within months.

Since syphilis was usually sexually transmitted, it was frequently carried by armies and their followers. It was first found in French armies invading Italy in the 1490s. The Italians called it the "French pox," while the French called it "the Neapolitan disease," and the Neapolitans "the Spanish disease." A common treatment was the application of mercury to the open sores, which had the effect of poisoning the patient.

## SMALLPOX

There was also no effective cure for smallpox, of which there were frequent epidemics across Europe in the 16th century. The virus was spread by direct or indirect contact with an infected person. It could survive for months in textiles or dust in a sickroom. By 1700 it was killing more people than any other disease. Its symptoms were a high fever and pustules that left survivors with disfiguring marks on the skin.

In the early 16th century smallpox and other diseases were carried by Europeans to the New World. They rapidly decimated the native population of Mexico and South America, which had no immunity to these new diseases.

Diseases and epidemics were commonly regarded as a sign of God's displeasure. As a result, praying, fasting, and moral improvements were often seen as the best response. The Italian physician Girolano Fracastoro (1478–1553) recognized that smallpox and other diseases were contagious and, in an early version of germ theory, proposed that they were spread by minute bodies. However, his theory did not lead to the discovery of any effective cures.

SEE ALSO
• Anatomy
• Daily life
• Exploration
• Medicine and surgery

# SIKHISM

**The Sikh religion developed in the Punjab in northern India between the late 15th and late 17th centuries. Its founder was the guru, or religious teacher, Nanak, who attracted followers with a system of beliefs that combined elements from Hinduism and Islam.**

There had already been several attempts to reconcile Hinduism and Islam before Nanak (1469–1539) (*see box p. 15*). However, following the Mogul invasion of northern India in 1398, much of the work of reconciliation had come undone. The invasion led local rulers to give up their allegiance to the Muslim sultan in Delhi and establish their own power bases. Most of the local rulers were Muslim themselves and began to persecute the Hindus in their regions. It was into this unstable, divided society that Nanak was born on April 15, 1469, in a village in western Punjab, in northern India.

### GURU NANAK

When he was 30, Nanak had a mystical experience in which he heard God's voice telling him to go into the world and teach people how to pray. He spent the rest of his life traveling in India and West Asia, establishing communities of followers wherever he went. These followers were known as Sikhs, from the Sanskrit word for "disciple."

Nanak wanted to unite Hindus and Muslims. He promoted monotheism, or the belief in one God. He also condemned the caste system, the Hindu social hierarchy that placed indigenous peoples at the lowest level. Nanak preached his message in a simple way that anyone could understand. He taught that God was a spiritual concept on which the principles of correct behavior rested. For example, he defined God as truth and said that anyone who did not tell the truth was behaving in an ungodly manner. He also taught that all humans have the potential for goodness within them, but that most people are blind to this capacity and instead fill their lives with *maya* (illusion). This belief influenced the role of the guru in Nanak's teachings. The guru was to act as a spiritual guide, diverting people from the path of *maya* and making them aware of their basic goodness.

*A princely ruler pays respect to Nanak (dressed in white), the spiritual leader and founder of Sikhism, in this 16th-century painting.*

# THE BHAKTI MOVEMENT AND THE SUFIS

Many of Guru Nanak's teachings were a synthesis of earlier movements that had originated in Hinduism and Islam. The Hindu Bhakti movement emphasized unity with Islam by promoting monotheism, in contrast with the Hindu belief in many different deities. The most famous Bhakti teachers were Ramanuja (about 1016–1137) and Kabir (1440–1518), who described himself as the child of Rama (a Hindu deity) and Allah (the Arabic word for God). A number of Islamic mystics and religious scholars, the Sufis, meantime sought to convert followers to Islam through peaceful means. Like the Bhakti movement, the Sufis opposed the Hindu caste system and consequently attracted many converts from the poorer levels of Hindu society.

*The Golden Temple in the city of Amritsar is the principal place of worship for Sikhs. The original temple was built in 1604; the present structure dates from the 1800s.*

Nanak was the first of the 10 Sikh gurus. The centers he founded throughout India and Asia did not last long after his death, but under the leadership of the next four gurus Sikhism began to establish itself as a major faith in the Punjab. Beside attracting new followers, the four gurus all made individual contributions to the religion's development.

The second guru, Angad (1504–1552), devised a new written script with which he wrote down all the hymns and prayers of Nanak. The third guru, Amar Das (1479–1574), appointed local agents called *masands* to help organize worship and collect offerings that were used to build temples and spread the faith. The fourth guru, Ram Das (1534–1581), established a new settlement that was destined to become the Sikh capital, Amritsar, while the fifth guru, Arjun (1563–1606), organized the building of the main temple in Amritsar and compiled the writings of all the gurus since Nanak, as well as contributions from Hindu and Muslim writers, in the Granth Sahib (Holy Volume).

## DEFENDING THE FAITH

While the first five gurus preached a peaceful message that was designed to appeal to both Muslims and Hindus, the next five led Sikhism in a more militant direction. The success of the Sikhs under the third guru, Amar Das, had aroused the opposition of other

groups, such as the Hindu Brahmin priests, but the tolerance shown toward Sikhism by the Mogul Emperor Akbar (ruled 1556–1605) had helped maintain its growth. Under Emperor Jahangir (ruled 1605–1627), however, this tolerance came to an end. Jahangir resented the growing popularity of the Guru Arjun and had the guru arrested and imprisoned. Arjun died in prison on May 30, 1606.

The sixth guru, Hargobind (1595–1644), set the trend for Sikhism in the 1600s by raising a defensive army and building a fortress in Amritsar. To avoid persecution, Hargobind and Har Rai (1630–1661), the seventh guru, retreated into the Himalayan foothills. Sikhism continued to attract followers, largely because its more assertive attitude appealed to Punjabis who wanted to define themselves as a distinct national group.

The eighth guru, Hari Krishen (1656–1664), died of smallpox at the age of eight after having appointed his great uncle Tegh Bahadur (1621–1675) as his successor. At around the same time, Emperor Aurangzeb (ruled 1658–1707) began to persecute both Hindus and Sikhs in northern India. Efforts by Tegh Bahadur to encourage resistance to the persecution enraged Aurangzeb. He summoned the guru to Delhi and had him beheaded on November 11, 1675.

### THE LAST GURU

Once again the untimely death of a guru spurred the Sikhs to build up their military strength. The tenth guru, Gobind Singh (1666–1708), organized another army and built more fortresses across the Punjab. He tried to reconcile the pacifism of the first five gurus with the more warlike attitudes of the later gurus, holding that it is just to resist an enemy who seeks one's destruction.

Gobind Singh also introduced major reforms designed to make the Sikh community more disciplined and stable. He believed that the institution of living gurus led to arguments about who would succeed whom and declared that he was to be the last guru. He also regarded the institution of local agents, the *masands,* to be corrupt and decided to abolish it. Gobind Singh announced that the sacred Sikh book the Granth Sahib should take the place of the guru; the *masands* were to be replaced with an already established institution of elected representatives, the *panth.*

In 1699 Gobind Singh proclaimed a new community within Sikhism: highly disciplined followers known as the Khalsa ("the pure"). These Sikhs were to be distinguished from others by outward signs, such as never cutting the hair on their heads or bodies. The tenth and last guru died in October 1708, murdered by two men who were believed to be connected to an imperial commander. His reforms, however, helped revitalize Sikhism and helped it withstand continued hostility from Mogul emperors in the early 1700s.

*This photo shows the huge Badshahi Mosque in Lahore, Pakistan, which was built between 1672 and 1674 for Emperor Aurangzeb. The emperor tried to enforce conformity on Islam and had the Sikh Guru Tegh Bahadur executed. The white building in the foreground is the mausoleum of Ranjit Singh, who founded a Sikh kingdom in the Punjab in the first half of the 19th century.*

SEE ALSO
- India
- Islam

# SLAVE TRADE

The two centuries between 1500 and 1700 saw the rise of the Atlantic slave trade, which supplied the colonies of the American mainland and the Caribbean with African slaves. By the end of the 1800s the trade had forcibly transported between nine and 10 million Africans to America.

Slavery and the slave trade already had a long history by the 1500s. Both had been major features of ancient Roman society, although slavery had declined in Europe with the demise of the Roman Empire in the fifth century. Elsewhere, in the seventh and eighth centuries Arab Muslims conquered North Africa and took over that region's slave trade. They supplied Arab cities in the Mediterranean region and West Asia with black slaves from West Africa. The Arabs tapped into Africa's long-established slave tradition, in which one society took slaves from another in raids or as the spoils of war.

Slavery also existed in medieval Europe. Between the eighth and 10th centuries Germans captured and enslaved large numbers of Slavs from eastern Europe; the word "slave" is derived from the word Slav. Between the 10th and 13th centuries the Italian city-states of Genoa and Venice also traded in and enslaved Slavs, as did the Africans, Greeks, and Italians.

### THE PORTUGUESE TRADERS

It was the Portuguese, however, who stepped up European involvement in slavery. In the early 1400s Portuguese explorers began mapping the African coastline south of the Sahara Desert. Their main aim was to discover gold, but in the quest to finance their explorations, they began to trade slaves

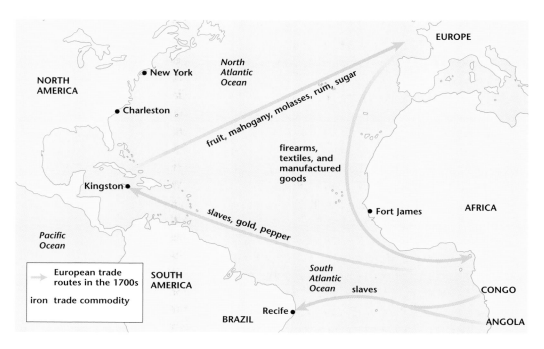

*This map shows the triangular trade in which slave traders carried different cargoes on different legs of the journey. Slaves were carried on the so-called Middle Passage.*

# THE MIDDLE PASSAGE

The Middle Passage is the term used to refer to the African slaves' journey by ship across the Atlantic Ocean to the Americas. So called because it described the part of the process of enslaving people after their capture but before being sold, it has become a byword for the cruelty and suffering that millions of Africans endured. During the voyage, which lasted between 20 and 90 days, slaves were chained to the floor, lying row upon row on platforms that were themselves stacked in tiers. They could neither stand nor turn over, although, if the weather was good, the crew would exercise them on deck. They ate twice a day; but if a crossing took longer than expected, rations were severely reduced, leading to starvation. While it was not in anyone's interest for slaves to die on the crossing—ship captains only got paid for live slaves—the attitude that the Africans were less than human led to appalling mistreatment. Historians estimate that death rates on the Middle Passage averaged around 13 percent but could be higher than 20 percent.

as well. Portugal's activities ended the Arab monopoly on the slave trade. Initially there was little difference between the Christian and Islamic trades. Both supplied slaves to mainland Europe, the Mediterranean, and West Asia; in both cases slaves were mostly used in domestic service.

Between 1450 and 1550, however, the Portuguese developed a system that used vast numbers of Africans as slaves on plantations abroad. The first Portuguese plantations were on the Atlantic islands of the Azores, Madeira, and São Tomé. The islands were ideal for the cultivation of sugar, but there was a labor shortage in mainland Europe due to slow population growth. The Portuguese therefore imported Africans to work in the sugar fields. Initially, plantation owners used a mixture of African slaves and wage laborers; but by the mid-1500s São Tomé, by then the biggest sugar producer, relied solely on a workforce made up of around 6,000 enslaved Africans.

### NATIVE AMERICAN SLAVES
The discovery and settlement of the Americas by Europeans led to a colossal increase in the trade in African slaves. At first the Spanish, who conquered Mexico and large parts of South America in the 1500s, used native peoples to cultivate their American lands and to mine for silver and gold. However, many natives died from contracting European diseases, as well as from the intensive labor they were forced to undertake.

Other factors made the Spanish reconsider how they would work their American lands. Many native peoples in the Spanish Empire resented their exploitation at the hands of the conquerors and from time to time rose

*Spanish conquistadors use enslaved Native Americans to carry supplies on an expedition in this 16th-century illustration. European diseases and enslavement decimated native populations.*

*This late 17th-century illustration shows punishments and mutilations inflicted on slaves in the French colony of Martinique. Slaves had few rights and suffered brutal treatment from their owners.*

up against them, threatening Spanish property and lives. Furthermore, many Spanish believed that it was wrong to enslave the very people they were attempting to convert to Christianity. They included Bartolomé de las Casas (1474–1566), the bishop of Chiapas in Mexico. In 1537 he returned to Spain and asked Charles V, the Holy Roman emperor and Spanish king, to consider shipping African slaves to the Americas as an alternative to enslaving Native Americans. Charles agreed and issued a license to allow each Spanish colonist to import 12 African slaves.

### THE ATLANTIC TRADE

At first Portuguese traders supplied Africans to the Spanish Americas. After the unification of Spain and Portugal in 1580 Spain used Portugal's slave market for its own ends. By 1650 up to 300,000 African slaves had been sent to the Spanish Americas, most to Peru and Mexico. They were mainly used to mine gold and silver but also worked in vineyards, sugar plantations, cattle ranches, and other concerns.

The Portuguese were much slower to settle their own South American territory, Brazil, but by the mid-1500s they realized that sugar was the ideal crop to make the colony profitable. At first they relied on natives to work on the new plantations, but a smallpox epidemic in the 1560s severely reduced the labor force. Having already successfully used African slaves on their plantations on the Atlantic islands, the Portuguese turned to Africa for their replacement labor. By 1630 there were some 170,000 African slaves in Brazil.

### MORE NATIONS JOIN THE TRADE

By the 17th century other European countries were challenging Spanish and Portuguese dominance in the Americas. In 1630 the Dutch seized Recife and Pernambuco in Brazil. In 1638 they captured Portuguese settlements on the west coast of Africa, giving them access to supplies of slaves and ports from which to ship them across the Atlantic.

At the same time, the French and the English established colonies on the east coast of North America and in the Caribbean. Unlike the Spanish a century before, they had fewer natives to use for labor and so for the first half of the 17th century shipped out poor European workers (*see box p. 20*). The

*Comme, les Portuguais fouettent leurs Esclaves lors quils ont deserté.*

*Invention d'un François de la Martinique.*

*This painting from the mid-1630s shows a slave market in Brazil. In the 17th century around two million Africans were forcibly transported to Brazil and the Caribbean, where traders sold them as slaves mainly to the owners of sugar plantations.*

situation of these laborers differed little from that of the African slaves. The poor, both black and white, united in Bacon's Rebellion of 1675–1676 in Virginia. The ruling colonists realized they had to gain the support of poor whites against poor blacks to prevent further uprisings. They did this by granting favors and privileges to poor whites, marking the start of the transition to racial slavery.

As sugar plantations were set up on the Caribbean islands, increasing numbers of Africans were imported to work there. English-owned Barbados had 6,000 African slaves before the first plantations were developed in 1645. By 1680, when sugar had become a major feature of the island's economy, 38,000 slaves were working in its fields.

## THE PEAK IN ATLANTIC TRADE

By 1700 more than 450,000 Africans had been sent to the Caribbean as slaves. In contrast, by the same year French and English colonists in North America had imported fewer than 30,000 African slaves. This situation was to change drastically in the 1700s, when vast numbers of slaves were used on tobacco and cotton plantations. By the 1780s, the peak of the Atlantic slave trade, some 80,000 Africans were brought to the Americas each year.

## INDENTURED LABOR

In the 1600s many poor white Europeans crossed the Atlantic to work on farms and plantations in the Caribbean and North America. Most could not afford the cost of the voyage and so entered into indentured contracts with plantation owners and other settlers. In return for their passage individuals agreed to serve their sponsor for between three and five years, after which they would be freed and given several acres of land. The system was frequently abused, and indentured workers were often treated worse than slaves. Because indentured laborers did not belong to a master for life, masters had even less incentive to care for them. Many servants died before completing their contract.

SEE ALSO

- Africa
- Agriculture
- Colonization
- Latin America
- Native Americans
- North America
- Servants
- Sugar
- Tea and coffee
- Textiles
- Tobacco
- West African states
- West Indies

# SOCIAL ORDER

During the 16th and 17th centuries European society continued to be rigidly hierarchical, divided into different social groups with differing powers and privileges. However, wider political, economic, and religious changes affected these traditional relationships and balances of power.

Since the Middle Ages most Europeans had a standard view of society in which people belonged to one of three broad social groups: the clergy, nobility, or the commons. In a period when the Christian faith dominated life, people believed that this division of society was ordained by God. The clergy were considered the most important group because they spread God's word and attended to people's spiritual needs; next in importance came the nobility, wealthy men who took up arms to defend Christianity. Last of all came the commoners, who accounted for the vast majority of the population. Their role was to provide for and support the clergy and nobility.

### NOBLES, CLERGY, COMMONERS

In reality the situation was far more complex. Each of these broad social groupings contained a huge range and diversity of people. The clergy included highly educated men, many from noble or wealthy merchant families, who became bishops and prelates (high-

*Crowds watch as Thomas Wentworth, earl of Strafford, is executed on Tower Hill, London, in 1641. Public executions were intended to serve as an example to others of the consequences of criminal behavior.*

A. Doctor Vsher Lord Primate of Ireland,
B. the Sherifes of London,
C. the Earle of Strafford,
D. his kindred and Friends.

ranking churchmen) and enjoyed a privileged lifestyle similar to that of princes. It also comprised monks and friars, as well as poor village priests, some of whom were barely literate.

Most of the nobility, who made up the ruling classes, came from long-established families whose wealth and power was based on the large estates they owned. The most important members of the nobility were royalty. Then came the nobles who served them: the princes, knights, and lords who raised and commanded armies on the monarch's behalf, and the courtiers who advised them on policy matters and worked in the growing royal bureaucracies. In turn these aristocrats and courtiers exercised power over a whole network of lesser nobles and local landowners.

Most commoners were peasants and artisans. In the 16th century some 80 to 90 percent of Europeans lived in the countryside. The vast majority of them were peasants who lived off the land, growing and producing enough crops and food for their families to survive.

### SOCIAL TIES AND DUTIES

Most land and wealth, and with them political power, was concentrated in the hands of the nobility. The Catholic church was also a major landowner and exercised direct influence on the lives of people across Europe. Commoners were bound to these two privileged social groups by various ties of obligation and duty.

Landowners had direct control over peasants who worked their land. The tenure, or land-holding, agreements that linked the two varied. Some peasants paid their landlord an annual rent for their land. These rents were commonly paid in kind, in the form of farm produce or labor for the lord. Other peasants were bound by

sharecropping. Under this system the landlord provided his tenant with seed and livestock with which to farm; in return the tenant had to give the landlord a proportion of his produce.

The lords had duties to peasants in return for their fulfilment of tenurial agreements. They were meant to maintain justice and order, as well as to protect their tenants in times of war and to show them mercy in times of hardship, such as famines.

### TITHES AND TAXES

Peasants were similarly bound to the Catholic church through tithes. Under this ancient system they had to provide the church with a proportion of their crops every year. Tithes were used to support the clergy, maintain and build churches, and to assist the poor.

Peasants were also obliged to pay the state taxes. They and other

*The Spanish Saint Diego of Alcalá prays among the poor in this painting by the 17th-century artist Esteban Murillo. Poverty was widespread in the 16th and 17th centuries, and people regarded giving charity to the poor as a Christian duty.*

# SOCIAL OUTCASTS AND OUTSIDERS

In countries across Europe some people were treated as if they had no place in the accepted social order. These outsiders included religious and ethnic minorities such as Jews, Muslims, and Roma (gypsies). They were not allowed to live in certain areas, patronize certain establishments, or enjoy the benefits of certain institutions. If they were living in poverty, for example, they were not entitled to charity. In many cases they were expelled from cities and countries.

People from religious and ethnic minorities were not the only ones to suffer persecution. In a superstitious age anyone who did not conform to existing social standards attracted suspicion and was blamed for misfortunes that befell the community. Single adults, particularly women, were often accused of being in league with the devil and inflicting evil. Thousands of them, mainly women, were killed for practicing witchcraft in the 1500s and 1600s.

*Peasants present their ruler with game in this Italian painting made sometime between about 1580 and 1640. Peasants were obliged to give produce to the lord whose land they farmed, as well as to the church, which often left them with little to live on themselves.*

commoners—who lacked the political power of the nobility—were often the most heavily taxed members of society. Taxes provided money to finance government and wars. As monarchs engaged in ever more large-scale and costly warfare in the 16th and 17th centuries, levels of taxation rose.

### UPSETTING THE BALANCE

The burden of rents, tithes, and taxes meant that the poor often struggled for survival. Excessive taxation led to unrest and sometimes popular rebellion, as happened in the Spanish kingdom of Naples in 1648. Natural disasters such as crop failures, epidemics, and famines—and manmade ones, such as wars—led to widespread death, poverty, and hunger, wiping out large swaths of the population.

Indeed, population changes also had implications for social order. In the 15th and 16th centuries, for example, there was a general increase in the population, which meant more mouths to feed and an increase in the number of landless laborers, who relied on wages to buy their food. In real terms food prices rose, and wages dropped.

More and more people fell into poverty. In some regions landowners increased their landholdings at the expense of peasants. In Poland and northern Germany, for example, nobles consolidated vast estates to provide produce to the growing European markets. At the same time, they reduced the status of peasants who worked their land to serfdom— imposing on them increased labor services and restricting their freedom. In England from the 1500s landowners began to enclose land, which denied peasants the right to graze their animals on common land.

### THE GROWTH OF TOWNS

The growth of towns also affected social order. Urbanization took place as trade began to flourish in the Middle

Ages, and the number of towns continued to grow in the 16th and 17th centuries. Although by 1700 only about 15 percent of the population lived in towns, and the towns were generally quite small, they were nonetheless economically powerful.

Economic prosperity brought political power—and sometimes independence—to towns. In some regions this led to friction between the authorities of burgeoning towns and the landed nobility. Almost everywhere, however, land rather than money remained the marker of social status: Successful professionals invested their money in country estates.

### THE PROTESTANT CHALLENGE

The greatest challenge to the accepted order of society in the 16th century came from the Protestant Reformation. Reformers such as Martin Luther (1483–1546), Huldrych Zwingli (1484–1531), and John Calvin (1509–1564) attacked as corrupt the beliefs, rituals, and hierarchy of the Roman Catholic church, which for centuries had been the foundation on which all levels of European society was based.

Protestantism appealed to different people for different and sometimes complex reasons. Its attraction was often linked to dissatisfaction with existing social, economic, and political conditions. In the German Peasants' War (1524–1525), for example, support of the reformed faith was combined with the wider desire of villages, towns, and regions for independence and freedom from growing lordly controls.

Protestantism also attracted noble and royal followers, many of whom used it in their struggles for increased power and authority. Religion became a part of wider political and dynastic struggles. France was torn apart by bitter conflict between Catholics and

Huguenots (Protestants) in the second half of the 16th century, and the Thirty Years' War (1618–1648), which wreaked havoc across Europe, was fueled by religious differences.

### INCREASING ROYAL POWER

The adoption of Protestantism was also part of a broader consolidation of royal power that took place in the 1500s and 1600s. Monarchs who adopted the new religion saw the renunciation of Catholicism as a way of strengthening their own position. They no longer had to accept the supreme authority of the pope or the special laws and privileges by which the clergy lived. The national churches that they created strengthened their own position as well as their subjects' sense of nationhood.

*The sick line up to be cured by King Charles II of England in this 1684 picture. People believed that the monarch was so powerful his touch could cure diseases.*

SEE ALSO
- Clergy
- Courts and courtiers
- Crime and punishment
- Popular rebellions
- Reformation
- Towns
- Wealth and poverty

# SOUTHEAST ASIA

**Rich in natural resources—most notably spices—Southeast Asia was at the center of a vast trading network stretching from China to Europe. The arrival of European merchants in the 16th century had a major effect on the region's trade but not initially on its political makeup.**

The borders of kingdoms and empires within Southeast Asia had constantly changed in the centuries before 1500. The states that had emerged in the region—covering what are now Myanmar (Burma), Thailand, Cambodia, Laos, Vietnam, Singapore, Malaysia, Indonesia, and the Philippines—had traditionally been dominated by their neighbors, India to the west and China to the east. Indian influence had declined from the late 13th century. However, under the Ming Dynasty, which had come to power in 1368, the Chinese had increased their trade with the region, establishing many settlements along the coasts.

## RELIGION IN SOUTHEAST ASIA

In 1511 Portuguese mariners, who were determined to seize control of the region's trade, captured Melaka on the west coast of the Malay Peninsula. With the Europeans came Christianity to compete with the traditional regional faiths of Hinduism and Buddhism, and the more recently established Islam. The Islamic faith had been brought by Arab merchants to Aceh in northwest Sumatra at the end of the 13th century. From here it had spread to the rest of Sumatra, the Malay Peninsula, parts of Borneo, and Java and other islands within what is now Indonesia.

Among the many peoples of Southeast Asia there were some, such as the Cham of Vietnam, the Khmer of Cambodia, and the Mon of Burma, who had been long settled in the region. Others, such as the Tai of Thailand and the Javanese, were comparative newcomers. The Tai, for example, had been forced out of southwest China in the eighth century. They moved into Thailand, conquering kingdoms already established there.

*These images of Buddha are in a Thai temple in Petchaburi, with murals from the time of the kingdom of Ayutthaya (about 1350–1767).*

The region as a whole prospered from local and international trade—much of it carried on maritime routes in the South China Sea and across the Indian Ocean. Basic foodstuffs, such as rice and dried fish, were traded as well as high-value commodities such as precious stones or the rare woods and spices that grew on the Spice Islands of the Moluccas and the Malay Peninsula.

## KINGDOMS OF SOUTHEAST ASIA

There were five major powers in the region at the beginning of the 16th century: Myanmar, Vietnam, Ayutthaya in Thailand, Majapahit on the island of Java, and Melaka.

In central Myanmar the Shan people under the Toungoo Dynasty had conquered other peoples to create a kingdom whose capital was Ava. The dynasty reached its high point in the late 16th century under the ruler Bayinnaung (ruled 1551–1581). An outstanding military commander, Bayinnaung extended Myanmar's dominance east toward the state of Chieng Mai and south to Ayutthaya in Thailand and into Laos.

In Vietnam what is called the Later Le Dynasty (to distinguish it from an earlier dynasty of the same name) had come to power in 1428 after a successful military campaign to drive the Chinese out of the north of the country. In the south it conquered the Indian-influenced kingdom of Champa in 1471. However, the Le emperors placed too much power in the hands of feudal lords. After one temporarily usurped the throne in 1523, the real government of the state was divided between the Trinh family in the north and the Nguyen family in the south. By 1630 the country had been split by two walls built by the Nguyen across the plain of Dong Hai. It would not be reunited until the 18th century.

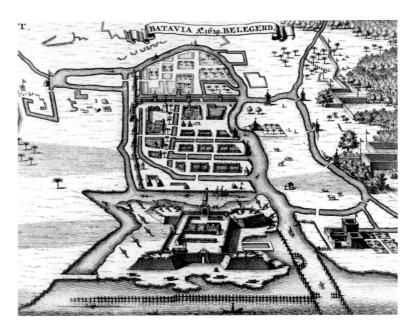

In Thailand the Tai people of the southern kingdom of Ayutthaya—known by their neighbors as the Siamese—had conquered the Tai Empire of Sukothai in the mid-15th century. From the capital city of Ayutthaya, north of what is now Bangkok, the Siamese ruled over much of north-central Thailand and its southern peninsula. The kingdom of Ayutthaya inherited many Hindu practices from the Khmer capital of Angkor, in present-day Cambodia, which the Siamese sacked in 1431. Among them was a social hierarchy similar to that of India, under which everyone had duties that they were obliged to carry out for their superiors.

## TRADING CENTER

At the beginning of the 16th century Ayutthaya was a trading center that attracted many merchants from, among other countries, Portugal, China, India, and Persia. Although Ayutthaya was conquered by a Toungoo force from Myanmar in 1569, it soon recovered its independence. In the late 17th century—after Dutch, English, Spanish, and French traders had made

*Batavia (now Jakarta) in 1629, 10 years after it was founded by the Dutch as the capital of their trading empire in Southeast Asia. It was planned in the style of Dutch cities, with canals lined on each side by fine buildings.*

# BATAVIA

The capital of the Dutch East Indies, Batavia was founded in 1619 by Governor General Jan Pieterszoon Coen on a site in Java where the Dutch had previously established a trading post. They initially built a fortress, but this soon became a walled settlement that withstood numerous attacks by local rulers. For 200 years the town's focal point continued to be the company fortress and the waterfront warehouses where the merchants stored goods that were to be shipped to Europe.

Coen envisioned Batavia as an Asian version of Amsterdam, complete with canals. To some extent his dream was realized. Throughout the 17th century Batavia attracted settlers and became a flourishing colonial capital with fine buildings in the Dutch colonial style. Its commer-

cial influence reached as far as India in the west and China and Japan in the east. The city was dubbed the "Queen of the East." By the 18th century, however, the city was also known as the "white man's graveyard." Its swamps and canals attracted mosquitos that carried malaria, which killed thousands of European settlers.

In the 19th century the Dutch set about draining the swamps and canals. As they succeeded, the city acquired another nickname: "Pearl of the Orient." It remained in Dutch hands until World War II (1939–1945), when it was briefly occupied by the Japanese, who renamed the city Jakarta, a shortened version of its old Javanese name. When Indonesia became independent in 1949, Jakarta became the national capital.

*Portuguese and Dutch fleets fight for control of trade in Southeast Asia. The Dutch secured victory in 1641 with their capture of Melaka on the Malay Peninsula.*

an impact in Siam—King Narai (ruled 1656–1688) sent ambassadors to the French court at Versailles. Eventually, however, the efforts of European missionaries to convert Buddhists to Christianity provoked the Siamese to expel the French in 1688 and later to effectively cease contact with Europe for around 150 years.

The Majapahit kingdom that had dominated the island of Java for 300 years was in decline by 1500. The Indianized, Hindu-Buddhist kingdom faced competition from new Islamic states that were founded on the northern coast of the island in the late 14th and early 15th centuries. A hundred years or so later the new states had eclipsed Majahapit power.

One of the major sources of Islamic influence in the region after around 1400 was Melaka on the Malay Peninsula. Melaka was a trading hub and reflected the trend in Southeast Asia—particularly in Java—toward urbanization. In the early 16th century the city had a population of around 100,000 people, more than most European cities of the time. However, Melaka's dominance was shortlived. In 1511 it was conquered by a Portuguese force led by Afonso de Albuquerque.

### EUROPEAN INFLUENCE
The arrival of the Portuguese heralded European involvement in maritime trade in the region. Albuquerque's aim

was to gain a Portuguese monopoly on the lucrative spice trade with Europe. Portuguese merchants soon reached the East Indies and Siam, and later China and Japan. Like later European adventurers, the Portuguese were more concerned with ensuring favorable trade terms than with colonization. Like later Europeans, too, they were only able to assert their power with the help of local allies.

The Portuguese soon found their position challenged. In the late 1500s English and Dutch mariners visited the region. In 1600 the English created an East India Company to trade with Asia. Two years later the Dutch founded an East India Company that set out to control trade in Southeast Asia by both excluding other Europeans and controling local Asian traders. From 1636 Governor General Jan Pieterszoon Coen used superior military power to lay the foundations of Dutch imperial power in Indonesia

from the Dutch colonial capital of Batavia in Java (*see box p. 27*).

As the Dutch expanded their influence, they were soon drawn into conflict with local rulers and with other European powers. In one notorious incident in 1623 the Dutch authorities in Amboina in the Moluccas executed 10 Englishmen, 10 Japanese, and one Portuguese on suspicion of plotting to assassinate the Dutch local governor. The incident, which the English called the Amboina Massacre, ended any chance of cooperation between the East India companies.

## DUTCH DOMINATION

The Dutch were now able to confine the English to a small base in Sumatra. In 1641 they confirmed their dominant role in the region by capturing Melaka from the Portuguese. They would consolidate their power in the 18th century, largely controlling the spice trade with Europe.

*French Jesuit missionaries arrive in the Buddhist kingdom of Siam (Thailand) in the 17th century. Their efforts to convert the Siamese to Christianity would eventually lead to their expulsion from the kingdom and the end of contact between Siam and Europe for over 150 years.*

SEE ALSO
- East India companies
- Islam
- Spices
- Trade

# SPAIN

Spain was the dominant power in Europe for most of the 16th century and part of the 17th century. Under the rule of the Hapsburg Dynasty it became the center of an empire that included the Netherlands and much of Italy, as well as vast territories in the Americas.

In 1500 Spain itself was a new nation. Fifty years earlier the Iberian Peninsula had been made up of several separate kingdoms. The marriage in 1469 of Isabella of Castile (ruled 1474–1504) and Ferdinand of Aragon (ruled 1479–1516) brought together the kingdoms of Castile and Aragon under their joint rule.

Ferdinand and Isabella added the Kingdom of Granada to Castile's territories when they conquered it from Moorish (North African) rule in 1492. They did not, however, unify Spain, instead allowing Castile and Aragon to retain their own separate institutions, including the cortes (parliaments).

## GROWTH OF ROYAL AUTHORITY

In Castile the monarchs asserted their authority over the powerful barons by removing the nobles from the royal administration and establishing a series of councils staffed by lawyers. They retained the good will of the barons, on whom they relied for their armies, by giving them titles, positions in the Catholic church, and important jobs in

## RELIGIOUS CONFORMITY

Spain had a racially and religiously diverse population. As well as the Catholic majority, it included sizable numbers of Jews, *conversos* (Jews who had converted to Christianity), Muslims (or Mudejars), and Moriscos (Muslims who had converted to Christianity). Ferdinand and Isabella's emphasis on religious conformity brought an end to the already waning toleration of these groups. *Conversos* were the first targets of the Inquisition. Then in 1492 a decree was issued that all Jews must convert to Christianity or leave the country. By 1500 the Mudejars faced the same decision. In the 1560s the treatment of the Moriscos in Granada led to a revolt (1568–1570), and in 1609 they were expelled. Such policies were socially divisive and economically damaging. For example, the expulsion of the Jews deprived Spain of many of its most economically active citizens, seriously affecting the growth of commerce and banking in the 16th century.

*Moors of Granada, defeated in 1492, pay tribute to the Catholic monarchs Ferdinand and Isabella.*

the various regions. Ferdinand and Isabella also enforced religious conformity (*see box p. 29*). They revived the Inquisition, a medieval religious court to stamp out heresy, and began to reform the Catholic church. These measures, continued by their successors, helped prevent Protestantism from becoming established in Spain.

In foreign policy Ferdinand tried to secure strategic points in North Africa to prevent Muslim raids on Spain. He also fought France for control of Italy. He was already king of Sicily and Sardinia, and in 1504 he recovered the Kingdom of Naples from French rule. More importantly, Isabella sponsored the explorer Christopher Columbus in his voyage of discovery to the Americas in 1492. He and the conquistadors who followed him claimed for Spain vast territories in the New World, including Mexico and much of Central and South America.

## THE HAPSBURG ERA

Ferdinand's death in 1516 marked a turning point in the history of Spain. Aragon and Castile were united under the rule of one king: Ferdinand's grandson, Charles I (ruled 1516–1556). Furthermore they became part of a much larger empire. Charles was a member of the powerful Hapsburg Dynasty, and he inherited vast lands, including the Netherlands, Luxemburg, Artois, Franche-Comté, and Austria in 1519. In 1519 he was also elected Holy Roman emperor as Charles V.

The first five years of Charles's reign were marked by a resurgence of traditional rivalries and power struggles in Spain. At first the young ruler, who spoke no Spanish, was unpopular. He had been raised in the Burgundian court of his grandparents, Maximilian I and Mary of Burgundy, and surrounded himself with Burgundian advisers. In Castile the towns rose up against him

*The conquistador Francisco Pizarro is commemorated by this statue in front of the church of San Martin in Trujillo, Spain. Pizarro conquered the Inca Empire on behalf of Spain in the 1530s. His conquests became part of the vast Spanish Empire in the New World.*

protecting his Italian kingdoms from Ottoman attack in the Mediterranean. His campaigns against the Ottoman Turks and the Protestants in the German states of the Holy Roman Empire appealed to the Spanish tradition of championing the Catholic faith. To many contemporaries the Holy Roman Empire and the Spanish Empire seemed one and the same.

### SPAIN'S GOLDEN AGE

In 1556 Charles handed to his son Philip II (ruled 1556–1598) the rule of Spain, its Italian colonies, Franche-Comté, and the Netherlands. He gave his Austrian lands to his brother Ferdinand, who also became Holy Roman emperor. Under Charles Spain had become the most powerful nation in Europe; under Philip it enjoyed what is often described as its golden age. Yet the constant and escalating military campaigns through which Spain asserted its dominance also contained the seeds of its collapse (*see box below*).

Philip made Madrid the permanent capital and further developed the council system of government. He also led reform of the Catholic church in

*This painting commemorates the Treaty of Cateau-Cambrésis agreed on by Henry II of France and Philip II of Spain in 1559. Under the terms of the treaty France recognized the supremacy of Spain in Italy.*

in the Comuneros Revolt of 1520 to 1521. However, the uprising was suppressed, and there were no more outright challenges to his authority. Although Charles spent only 16 years of his 39-year reign in Spain, he was successful in gaining the support of the nobles by continuing the system of patronage (gifts of offices) begun by Ferdinand and Isabella.

Charles also maintained many of his predecessors' policies. He continued Spanish offensives in North Africa and against the French in Italy. Charles also devoted increasing resources to

## BOOM AND BUST

One of the paradoxes of Spanish history in the 16th and 17th centuries is that while vast quantities of gold and silver poured in from Peru and Mexico, the Spanish government was in a perpetual state of bankruptcy. Royal spending on military campaigns far exceeded royal income. Charles I left Philip II with a debt of 36 million ducats. Philip II went bankrupt four times and left Philip III with a debt of 68 million ducats. So it went on.

The kings received income from a number of sources. One was the *quinta*, an import duty that entitled them to one-fifth of all gold and silver imported from the New World. Another was taxes granted by the cortes. Powerful nobles, particularly those in Aragon, refused to pay more taxes, and the growing burden of taxation fell increasingly on Castile and on the poorer members of society.

To obtain more money, the government sold bonds on which it then had to make interest payments to the purchaser. It also took out loans from German and Genoese banks run by wealthy families such as the Fuggers. In the 17th century the government debased the coinage, reducing the amount of precious metal in coins so that it could make a profit. This measure had the result of increasing prices (inflation). All these short-term measures only served to increase Spanish debts in the long run.

line with the recommendations of the Council of Trent (1545–1563). He inflicted defeats on France and secured Spain's dominion over Italy in the Treaty of Cateau-Cambrésis (1559). In 1568 he sent Spanish forces into the Netherlands to crush an uprising by Protestant rebels. In the Mediterranean Philip joined with the Venetians and the papal fleet to win a great symbolic victory over the Ottoman Turks at the Battle of Lepanto (1571). In 1580 he conquered Portugal, acquiring control of the whole Iberian Peninsula and the great Portuguese Empire.

Not everything went Philip's way. The revolt in the Netherlands escalated into a long-term war, and in 1588 the Spanish Armada—the fleet sent to attack England for supporting the Dutch rebels—suffered a crushing defeat. However, when Philip III (ruled 1598–1621) came to the throne, Spain still appeared to be the most dominant nation in Europe.

### DECLINING POWER

Under Philip III Spain dominated in a period of relative peace, having secured a treaty with England in 1604 and a 12-year truce with the Dutch rebels in 1609. Yet there were also signs of decline. Philip allowed a chief minister (*valido*) drawn from the aristocracy to take control of the government, which increased the power of the nobles. Spain was also crippled by a deepening financial crisis and owed its dominance less to its own strength than to the weakness of its main rival, France.

When the 16-year-old Philip IV (ruled 1621–1665) succeeded to the throne, his *valido*, the count de Olivares, pursued an aggressive foreign policy. He renewed hostilities with the Netherlands and involved Spain in the Thirty Years' War (1618–1648) in Germany and in war with France. His

resulting attempts to raise money and troops caused a revolt in Catalonia, in Aragon, in 1640. In the same year the Portuguese rebelled and reasserted their independence from Spain.

In 1648 Philip IV finally recognized the independence of the Dutch Republic (the present-day Netherlands) under the Treaty of Münster. In 1659 he signed the Treaty of the Pyrenees, which firmly established France as the dominant power in Europe. Spain then lost more lands to France, including Franche-Comté. The death of the last Spanish Hapsburg king, Charles II (ruled 1665–1700), plunged the nation into further turmoil as European rulers fought to secure the crown in the War of the Spanish Succession (1701–1714). Philip V, the grandson of the French King Louis XIV, was finally accepted as the new king, the first in the line of Bourbon kings of Spain.

*Philip III, king from 1598 to 1621, lacked the leadership qualities of his father.*

SEE ALSO

- Belgium and the Netherlands
- Charles V
- Counter Reformation
- Dynastic wars
- Fugger family
- Hapsburg family
- Inquisition
- Italian Wars
- Lepanto, Battle of
- Netherlands, Revolt of the
- Philip II
- Portugal
- Spanish Empire
- Taxes and government finances

# SPANISH EMPIRE

Spain began extending its territories overseas around the end of the 15th century. By 1600 it had carved out the most powerful empire on earth, covering huge regions of the Americas and extending out across Africa and the Pacific.

In 1469 Ferdinand V of Aragon (ruled 1479–1516) and Isabella of Castile (ruled 1474–1504) were married, the union drawing a previously disunited Spain under the joint rule of two monarchs. Having consolidated Spanish territory, Ferdinand and Isabella looked to the rest of the world. Their desire for empire had several roots. On its simplest level Spain wanted to expand into Asia to tap into

*This 16th-century book illustration shows Christopher Columbus landing on an island in the Bahamas, probably San Bartolomeo. Contact with Europeans was to prove fatal for the local people.*

the region's valuable metal, cloth, and spice trades. Looking south, meanwhile, Spain desired African colonies to protect Spanish maritime trade in the Mediterranean and Atlantic, to defend itself against Muslim raiders from North Africa, and to exploit Africa's supply of gold and slaves. Spain was also highly motivated by rivalry with its neighbor Portugal, which in 1488 had sent the explorer Batholomeu Dias (about 1450–1500) around the Cape of Good Hope at the southern tip of Africa and into the Indian Ocean, thereby opening up Asia to Portuguese expansion. In response Spain embarked on its own age of discovery in the late 1400s.

## THE NEW WORLD

Spain laid the foundations for its empire in 1492, when the Genoese navigator Christopher Columbus (1451–1506) set out on a Spanish-sponsored voyage to discover a westward maritime route to India and Asia. He actually discovered islands in the Caribbean. It was soon recognized that this was a "new" world between Europe and Asia, and Spain began claiming the territory for its own.

From 1492 to 1518 Spain colonized the Caribbean and began to explore

Central America, the Yucatan Peninsula, and the Gulf of Mexico. Colonial governors imposed Spanish rule on colonists and native people alike, and Spain began to gather taxes and goods from its territories. At first the Caribbean appeared to have limited commercial potential, but it provided a base for further exploration. Expanding the Spanish Empire would be the job of the conquistadors, military explorers toughened by wars at home with the Muslims. For the most part these men operated as independent agents without direct state support. In 1518 Hernán Cortés (1485–1547) led a band of conquistadors into Mexico, the territory of the Aztecs. Cortés conquered the entire Aztec Empire by 1521.

### FURTHER EXPANSION

Other explorers extended Spanish territory in different directions. The conquistador Francisco Pizarro (about 1475–1541) and his army pushed down through Peru, overwhelming the Inca peoples, killing their leader Atahualpa, and taking the Inca capital of Cuzco.

Further Spanish explorations extended Spanish territories as far as Patagonia, the southernmost portion of South America. In addition, John Cabot (about 1450–1499) explored South America's east coast and interior, while

*This map shows the extent of the Spanish Empire in America in 1625 and the major Native American empires that existed before the Spanish arrived. By the middle of the 16th century the Aztec and Inca empires had been devastated by Spanish conquistadors and the diseases they brought with them from Europe.*

# CONQUISTADOR CRUELTY

The conquistadors of Spain were brave soldiers, but they were also cruel to the native peoples. The Spanish Dominican missionary Bartolomé de las Casas (1474–1566) witnessed Spanish atrocities in the West Indies in around 1542. He wrote: "The Christians, with their horses and swords and lances began to slaughter and practice strange cruelty among them [the native peoples]. They penetrated into the country and spared neither children nor the aged, nor pregnant women, nor those in child labor, all of whom they ran through the body and lacerated, as

though they were assaulting so many lambs herded in their sheepfold."

In Guatemala in 1524 the conquistador Pedro Alvarado (about 1485–1541) oversaw the killing of around 24,000 Mayan civilians, and Hernán Cortés authorized the murder of 30,000 civilians of Cholula in 1519. In Spain the government was concerned about the power of the conquistadors and so reclaimed the right to govern local people. This led to wars between conquistadors and the royal authorities from the 1530s, the government only taking control of Peru in 1560.

# RELIGION AND EMPIRE

The Spanish often justified their empire as a means to spread Christianity. Missionaries accompanied the conquistadors and made many converts. Although the Christian message came in third place behind financial gain and political power in the Spanish Empire, the Catholic church did play an important role in the running of the colonies. Spanish priests founded schools for settlers' children and for native children throughout the Americas. They also made dictionaries of local languages and studied the natural history and societies of local areas, spreading the knowledge throughout Europe. Missionaries also established banking facilities for the local people. While Spain colonized the Americas, Native Americans blended their own religions with those of Catholicism.

*The National Palace in Mexico City. In 1521 Spanish conquistadors defeated the Aztecs and left little evidence of their empire remaining. Spanish colonists built the palace on the site of the Aztec King Montezuma's castle to reinforce their control of Mexico.*

Francisco de Orellana (about 1490–1546) navigated the Amazon River from the Andes to the Atlantic Ocean.

## RULING THE AMERICAS

By the 1550s Mexico, Florida, Cuba, Central America, and much of western South America were in Spanish hands. The territories were divided into viceroyalties, governed by viceroys who ruled for the king in his absence. The Viceroyalty of New Spain incorporated Mexico, Central America, and the Caribbean. The Viceroyalty of Peru covered the South American colonies.

The Spanish began to exploit American natural resources and local peoples. They put in place a system known as *encomienda*, in which a Spanish lord, the *ecomendero*, controlled a population of Native Americans who supplied the lord with labor and taxes. In return the natives were meant to receive Spanish protection, although in reality they were treated as slaves. The *ecomienda* was eventually replaced by systems known as the *repartimiento* (in Mexico) and *mita* (in Peru), which put native laborers under state control rather than the control of a single lord. Despite the changes, Native Americans would face centuries of exploitation at the hands of the Spanish. By contrast, the Spanish Empire became the

wealthiest territory in the world, particularly through gold and silver mining, agriculture (the Spanish introduced wheat, vineyards, sugar, cattle, and sheep into the Americas), and textile production.

### OTHER SPANISH COLONIES

Although the Americas were by far the largest region of the Spanish Empire, they were not the only territory to be colonized by the Spanish. In 1542 the Spanish laid claim to the Islas Filipinas—the Philippine Islands—and expeditions in the 1560s and 1570s turned the claim into actual rule. The Philippines were to be a Spanish possession for over 300 years, and they were a major trading area for Spanish commerce in Asia. Other Spanish Pacific possessions included the island of Guam, which was an important stopping-off point for ships sailing between South America and the Philippines and the Caroline Islands.

In Africa Spain never attained the power achieved by Portugal, France, and England. It did, however, establish outposts on the North African coast. In the 1500s these outposts included Melilla, Oran, Bejaïa, Tunis, Tripoli, and Ceuta. The African possessions served several purposes: They gave Spain greater security from piracy in the Mediterranean and Atlantic waters, providing safer access to fishing waters and important trade routes, and they also allowed Spain to take advantage of African slave labor.

### DECLINING FORTUNES

The Spanish Empire continued to expand into the 1700s, especially in North America, where its western territories eventually stretched north up to Alaska and east to the Mississippi River. However, during the late 1600s the empire began to decline. During

the 17th century the French, Dutch, and English had become more aggressive in colonizing the Americas. The Spanish colonies and shipping routes became increasingly vulnerable to attack and piracy. Furthermore, the native population, on which the Spanish relied for labor, was decimated by diseases introduced from Europe. It has been estimated that around 90 percent of the 1500 population of the Americas (approximately 50 million people) had died by 1650.

### SPAIN'S LEGACY

Around the mid-1600s the price of silver also collapsed, and Spain entered an economic recession, heightened by the devastation caused by the Thirty Years' War (1618–1648). The colonies were becoming expensive, and the Spanish government increasingly left colonial rule up to local officials, which in turn meant a reduction in profit for the Spanish homeland. With Spain steadily abandoning its colonial responsibilities, the Spanish-American culture developed more of its own identity. The empire would finally collapse in the late 1700s and early 1800s, but the Spanish legacy in the Americas is clear and present today.

*The ruins of a gate and walls are all that remain of San Ignacio Miní, a 17th-century Jesuit church in present-day Argentina. Standing at the edge of a vast tropical forest, the church was once the center of a thriving community led by Jesuit priests.*

**SEE ALSO**

- Africa
- Aztec Empire
- Colonization
- Columbus, Christopher
- Conquistadors
- Exploration
- Inca Empire
- Missionaries
- Spain
- Taxes and government finances
- Trade

# SPICES

In the 16th and 17th centuries spices from Asia played a large role in European eating habits and health care. Immensely valuable, spices were one of the main inspirations for the voyages of exploration and the expansion of international trade.

Before the 16th century spices were extremely rare and costly in Europe, and were used only by the very wealthy. They were so expensive because they had to be carried overland from India and the East Indies (now Indonesia), across Central and West Asia to ports on the Mediterranean Sea, where Italian merchants purchased them to ship to Europe. At each stage the spices were handled by intermediaries, all of whom added to the sale price. By the time the spices had reached Europe, their price had multiplied many times.

### THE SEA ROUTE TO THE EAST

By 1500 the Portuguese had found the sea route to East Asia and the Indian Ocean around Africa's southern tip, the Cape of Good Hope. This discovery allowed European merchants to trade directly with spice producers. During the 16th century the Portuguese controlled the supply of spices, which by 1600 made up over half of cargoes shipped to Europe. By the 17th century, however, the Dutch and English were competing with them, often violently, for a share in the enormously profitable trade. By 1680 the military strength and sturdy,

technologically advanced ships of the Dutch had enabled them to take control of the trade.

The Dutch were determined to make as much profit from the spice trade as possible, regardless of the cost to the spice producers. They controlled the amount of spices that were grown and available for sale, and were able to pay and charge whatever they wanted for them. The producers, who had been profitably trading spices for about 2,000 years before the arrival of the Europeans, were driven into poverty.

### USES OF SPICES

Spices were used as medicines. Every apothecary (or drug store) had a range of spices that were mixed in powders,

*A dissected nutmeg is illustrated in this 16th-century herbal, a medical treatise. Nutmeg was in great demand both as a medicine and as a food flavoring. Fashionable people carried silver nutmeg containers and graters in case they needed to add the spice to their food.*

pills, and plasters to treat a range of illnesses. For example, cinnamon was believed to help with breathing problems and to promote digestion. Mace and nutmeg were regarded as effective medicines for stomach complaints, seasickness, and bad breath. Cloves were used to restore memory loss and fight nausea and toothache.

Spices were also used to flavor everything from meat and fish to jams, wine, and desserts. During the 17th century wealthy people liked to eat dishes flavored with a mix of pepper, cinnamon, ginger, cloves, and sugar (considered a spice at that time). They also wore pomanders—apple-sized silver balls pierced with openings and filled with spices and perfumes—to ward off the smells produced by

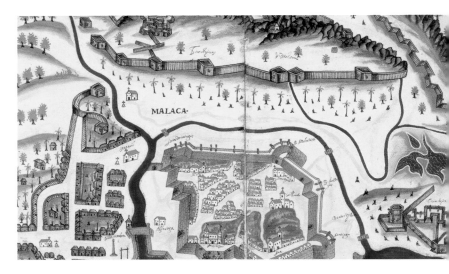

inadequate sanitation and unwashed bodies. The pleasant odors were believed to offer protection against the bad air that was thought to cause infectious diseases such as the plague.

*This 16th-century map is of Melaka, an important center for trading spices in present-day Malaysia. In 1511 the Portuguese took control of the city and its lucrative spice trade. The Dutch captured Melaka from the Portuguese in the 17th century.*

## THE SPICE CABINET

The main spices found in the spice cabinet of the 16th and 17th centuries were:

**Allspice**: With berries that taste like a combination of cinnamon, cloves, nutmeg, and pepper, allspice was discovered by the Spanish in Jamaica. When the English took over Jamaica in 1655, they increased trade in the spice.

**Cardamom**: One of the most expensive spices, cardamom was added to cookies and pastries to give them an exotic flavor.

**Cinnamon**: The perfumed bark of a tree native to Ceylon (Sri Lanka), cinnamon was widely used to flavor both sweet and savory dishes.

**Cloves**: Grown only on the Banda and Molucca Islands of the East Indies, cloves were used for flavoring, perfumes, and medicines. In Europe cloves cost three times the price of pepper.

**Ginger**: Before 1500 ginger was one of the most important spices in cooking, but its use became increasingly restricted to desserts.

**Grains of paradise**: Native to the coast of West Africa, these were also called Guinea, red, or cayenne peppers. Similar in taste to black pepper, they sold for about one-third of its cost.

**Nutmeg**: Native to the Moluccas, nutmeg was even more costly than cloves. Grated nutmeg was widely used in sweet dishes, and both the nut and the fibrous red netting surrounding it—mace—yielded expensive oils used to make perfume and drugs. In 1667 the Dutch settlement of New Amsterdam (New York) was traded to the English for a tiny nutmeg-producing island.

**Pepper**: Native to southwestern India and grown in Sumatra and Java in the East Indies, pepper was the most widely used spice in Europe. By the early 17th century Europeans were using around 3,000 tons of pepper a year.

**Saffron**: The stamens from the crocus flower were used mainly to color food an orangish-yellow. Grown in Europe, saffron was very expensive because of the time it took to gather.

**Vanilla**: From the seed pod of several species of orchids native only to Mexico, vanilla was mainly added to drinking chocolate.

**SEE ALSO**

- East India companies
- Food and drink
- Indonesia
- Sugar
- Trade

# SPINOZA, BARUCH

The 17th-century Dutch thinker Baruch Spinoza played a key role in the development of Western philosophy, particularly the line of thought known as rationalism. Many of his ideas were highly controversial, and his major writings were published only after he died.

Baruch Spinoza (1632–1677) was born in Amsterdam, the son of Portuguese Jews who had moved to the Netherlands in the late 1500s. From a young age he was a gifted scholar with a great appetite for learning. He was also a highly original thinker, and in 1656 his questioning of traditional Judaism led to his excommunication from the Amsterdam synagogue.

## LIFE AND WORKS

Spinoza earned his living as a maker of glass lenses while he continued to study philosophy and to develop his ideas. In 1660 he moved to Rijnsburg, near Leiden. There he wrote an abridgment (shortened version) of the *Principles of Philosophy*, a book by the French thinker René Descartes (1596–1650), who was the leading exponent of rationalism—an approach that holds that knowledge is based on concepts known through reason.

In 1664 Spinoza went to live in Voorburg and seven years later moved to The Hague. His aim was always to find the peace and quiet that he needed to think. He turned down a position at Heidelberg University in 1673 because he feared that it would restrict his intellectual freedom.

*Spinoza, shown here in a 17th-century portrait by a German artist, was famous during his own lifetime— he was visited by the influential German thinker Gottfried Leibniz—but his greatest influence came after his death, when his most important writings were published.*

Spinoza developed a precise and rigorous system of philosophy. He is best known for his pantheistic ideas, in which he equated God with the forces and laws of nature and the universe. His concept of an impersonal God was unpopular; it challenged traditional religious beliefs and was widely condemned. His *Theological-Political Treatise*, published anonymously in 1670, was widely attacked. Spinoza withheld publication of his greatest work, *Ethics Demonstrated in Geometrical Order*. It was only published by his friends after his death in 1677.

## SEE ALSO

- Descartes, René
- Leibniz, Gottfried
- Philosophy

# SPORTS, GAMES, AND PASTIMES

In the 16th and 17th centuries people of all ages from all classes of society amused themselves by practicing skills and taking part in games and competitions. While for children they were usually informal, for adults they often took the form of tournaments or other public displays.

Among the range of pastimes widely enjoyed were physical tests of strength and skill, games of chance, such as cards, and puzzles and word games. Theatrical performances and animal baitings, in which a large animal such as a bear was pitted against a number of dogs and made to fight until one or the other was dead, were also popular forms of entertainment.

Members of the nobility had additional sports to enjoy. Before the 16th century they often fought on the battlefield and were expected to be able to use swords and lances. They practiced by doing martial sports, such as jousting, fencing, and archery. As warfare increasingly required the use of cannons and muskets, the demand for militarily trained noblemen declined, and martial sports took on a new

*Noblemen display their prowess at a joust before an enthusiastic audience in Rome in 1610. The Italians were particularly fond of displaying the fine horsemanship that was a necessary part of jousting.*

of society, the conversational exchanges that demonstrated great cleverness with words. Courtiers were expected to have refined tastes in music, art, and poetry, and many cultivated an interest and a skill in the arts as artists, musicians, or poets. Courtiers sometimes circulated poetry among a coterie, or small group, of fellow courtiers.

Most members of the nobility—both men and women—were fond of hunting, a sport that was often forbidden to commoners. The animals most often hunted were deer, which were killed in enormous numbers all over Europe. Falconry, the practice of hunting with birds, was very popular, as was fishing.

### ENJOYMENT OF DANCING

People of all ranks enjoyed dancing. Everyone, from the monarch down to rural laborers, would dance at social gatherings. The type of dancing, however, differed depending on the social context. Courtly dances tended to involve intricate footwork and were performed by one or two couples. Country dances and other dances popular with the lower classes included several sets of couples, who together created round or rectangular patterns.

Many outdoor physical games required very few or no resources and so were popular among the poorer

*Noblemen play a 17th-century version of the modern game of billiards. A large table, cues, and balls were used, but the rules differed from those of today.*

significance as fashionable pastimes and popular spectator sports. Jousts, which required superior horsemanship as well as skills in wielding lances, were performed at public festivals mainly for entertainment.

Many members of the nobility, especially those who became courtiers to the monarch, devoted a great deal of time to what were referred to as games

## READING AS A PASTIME

Producing literature to entertain people became a commercial enterprise during the 16th and 17th centuries. Printed works of all types were sold to an ever-growing number of literate people. Political and religious tracts, short novels and long poems, the texts of plays, almanacs, histories, and other types of literature were enjoyed by all members of society. Pamphlets and single sheets called broadsides, which cost very little, were published for the mass market. Such pamphlets featured news of strange events, ballads, or other interesting information. A wealthier customer could purchase a more lavish item such as an illustrated book. Reading used to be a much more public activity than it is today. It was common, for example, for texts to be read out loud to groups of people.

members of society. Wrestling was common, as was soccer. At the time it was played not on a field with goalposts but in streets and meadows by boys or young men. The game was generally a free-for-all in which each player tried to get the ball for himself. There were no rules to prevent handling the ball or rough play, and serious injury could sometimes occur.

Physical games played by both boys and girls also tended to involve physical contact. In the English game of Hot Cockles, for example, a group of players would hit another player on the bottom. As they did so, the player who was hit would have to guess who was doing the hitting. When the player guessed correctly, he or she traded places with the identified hitter.

A rather less violent game was tennis, which was developed in France and played by men only. As the equipment and indoor court needed for tennis at this time were expensive, the game was played almost exclusively by the nobility. The lower classes played a modified version in which they used their hands instead of rackets. The Italian game of *bocce,* or bowls, was also popular with both men and women among the upper ranks. It involved tossing specially designed balls along an alley so that they landed as close as possible to a smaller ball.

### Indoor games

Table games such as chess, cards, early versions of backgammon, checkers, and cribbage were played by noblemen and noblewomen. Games played with dice were played by all orders of society. Some early board games were printed and marketed in the 16th century. The game of Goose, which was developed in continental Europe and exported to England, was based on a board with a track made up of squares. The players

would follow the squares in accordance with the numbers that came up on the dice that they rolled.

People also occupied themselves by telling each other jokes and riddles, some of which were printed in books, while others were improvised. The enjoyment of language was a part of musical entertainment. Singers put poetry to music and told stories in the form of musical ballads. Producing and listening to music with or without words was very popular. Wealthy people hired musicians to play for them. Others sang and played their own music.

### Criticism of game playing

In many Protestant countries games were associated with laziness and other vices. Puritans objected to dancing, watching plays, animal sports, and gambling, regarding them all as immoral, frivolous activities that should be banned. Despite the particularly negative attitude of some people toward gambling—also called gaming—the pastime was very popular. Bets were made on almost all kinds of games, including cards, outdoor sports, and animal sports. Even children made wagers, using such objects as polished pebbles for currency.

**The Cardsharps,** *painted by the Venetian artist Caravaggio in 1595, depicts two men tricking a young nobleman in a card game. Gambling with cards was extremely popular.*

SEE ALSO

- Children
- Courts and courtiers
- Daily life
- Drama
- Music
- Poetry

# STUART FAMILY

The Stuarts were the Scottish royal family who became monarchs of England from 1603, when King James VI of Scotland became King James I of England. The Stuarts then governed both countries until 1714, excluding the eleven years from 1649 to 1660.

The rule of the Stuart family began in Scotland in 1371. Over the next 300 years the claim of many of its members to the throne of Scotland and later to that of England was contested.

The family spelled its name as Stewart until 1558, when Mary Queen of Scots (ruled 1542–1567) married a French prince known as the Dauphin who later became King Francis II of France (ruled 1559–1560). The French do not pronounce the letter "w," so she changed the spelling of her last name to Stuart. When Mary returned from France in 1561, one year after her husband had died, she adopted the French spelling of her name, as did her descendants.

### VIOLENT ENDS

Many Stuarts suffered a violent death. King James I of Scotland (ruled 1406–1437), for example, was murdered at the command of a group of nobles, while James II, James III, and James IV (ruled 1488–1513) of Scotland all died in battle.

Mary Queen of Scots, who became queen in 1542 but only actually governed Scotland from 1561 to 1567, was deposed by her own subjects. A

*James VI of Scotland became James I of England in 1603. He hoped to achieve full political union of the two kingdoms but failed. The two countries finally united in 1707, during the reign of Queen Anne, the last Stuart monarch.*

Catholic in a country where Protestants were taking control of the government, she quickly became very unpopular. Her marriage in 1567 to the earl of Bothwell after he had been involved in the murder of her previous husband, Lord Darnley, led to her being deposed and fleeing to England.

Since Mary was a descendant of King Henry VII of England, she had a claim to the English throne and thus posed a threat to Queen Elizabeth I. As a result, Mary was imprisoned for 18 years before Elizabeth finally ordered her execution in 1587.

Because so many Stuart monarchs met early deaths, it was quite common for the Stuarts to come to the throne when they were still children. James II and James III became kings of Scotland before the age of nine and James IV at the age of 15. James V, Mary, and James VI of Scotland became monarchs before their third birthday, and regents ruled on their behalf for many years.

### STUART RULE IN ENGLAND

After a long period in which Queen Elizabeth refused to name a successor, she finally agreed that James VI of Scotland was her rightful heir. James, who was the son of Mary Queen of Scots, became king of Scotland in 1567, but he did not begin to claim any real power until 1581. When he ascended the English throne in 1603, he took the title of James I and set up court in London. He was joined there by many of his Scottish courtiers.

James knighted an unprecedented number of people, including numerous Scottish nobles. Unlike Elizabeth, he and his wife, Queen Anne, ran up large debts paying for luxurious clothing and entertainments. James insisted that the authority vested in the monarch was more important than that of Parliament, an attitude that sometimes caused much resentment.

At the same time, James did much to bring peace to his kingdom. He ended the wars with Ireland and Spain as well as the border wars between England and Scotland. James was also a scholar and wrote on various subjects including demonology, reflecting his support for witch hunting.

### DECLINE OF THE DYNASTY

James's son, King Charles I (ruled 1625–1649), inherited the large debts and Parliamentary resentment incurred by his father. He, too, could spend money frivolously, and his marriage in 1625 to the French Catholic princess

Henrietta Maria did little to endear him to his subjects. His relationship with Parliament became so difficult that he did not summon it at all between 1629 and 1640. His lack of political skills and his divisive policies led to civil war in 1642 and finally his execution in 1649.

The Scots proclaimed Charles I's son King Charles II in 1649. However, Charles was forced to flee to France after being defeated by an English Parliamentarian force. On finally ascending the throne in 1660, he adopted various strategies in his dealings with Parliament that undermined the power of the king. On his death in 1685 his brother James II inherited the throne. James was determined to revive Catholicism and rapidly alienated his subjects. He was deposed in 1689. His rule was followed by that of his daughter Mary and William III (ruled 1689–1702). James's daughter Anne (ruled 1702–1714) then became the last of the Stuart monarchs.

*The children of Charles I—the future kings Charles II and James II, and the princesses Mary, Elizabeth, and Anne—are portrayed in this painting. Charles I was a devoted family man, but Protestants in England disliked his Catholic wife.*

SEE ALSO
- Courts and courtiers
- England
- English Civil War
- English Revolution
- Glorious Revolution
- Scotland

# STUYVESANT, PETER

Peter Stuyvesant (about 1592–1672) was from 1647 the fourth and last director general of the Dutch colony of New Netherland, which was centered on New Amsterdam (now New York.) He greatly expanded the settlement beyond the southern tip of Manhattan.

The son of a church minister, Peter Stuyvesant was born in the Netherlands. Little is known of his early life, but by 1632 he was serving as a soldier in the Dutch West India Company. In 1644, while serving as governor of the Caribbean island of Curaçao, he lost a leg fighting the Portuguese on the island of Sint Maarten. From then on he had one wooden leg.

### STUYVESANT AS GOVERNOR

Stuyvesant was appointed director general of the Dutch colony of New Netherland and took up his post in 1647. His opposition to political and religious freedom soon made him unpopular. However, he introduced municipal government and a court of justice, and it was under him that the colony was formally named New Amsterdam on February 2, 1653. He also increased import taxes. He was responsible for the construction of Broadway, the town's main thoroughfare, the canal that became Canal Street, and the fortified defenses on Wall Street. In 1655 he conquered the small Swedish colony of New Sweden (on the Delaware River), naming it New Amstel, and incorporated it into New Netherland.

In a surprise attack in 1664 four English warships took control of New Amsterdam harbor. Their commander demanded that the Dutch surrender. Stuyvesant was defiant at first; but the other settlers were unwilling to support him, and he handed the colony to the English. He then lived quietly until his death on the Bouwerie, his farm in New York, after which the present-day Bowery district is named.

*A depiction of Stuyvesant landing in New Amsterdam in 1647.*

SEE ALSO

- Netherlands, Revolt of the
- New York
- North America

# SUGAR

**In 1500 sugar had long been one of the costliest luxury goods available in Europe. Over the next two centuries it remained affordable only by the wealthy, who used it as an ingredient in cough and cold medicines and as a flavoring for food and drink.**

Sugar was originally so costly in Europe because until the mid-15th century, it was imported only from Islamic lands on the shores of the Mediterranean where the hot climate was good for growing sugar cane. The Muslims learned how to produce sugar when they conquered Persia (present-day Iran) in the seventh century. The Persians in turn had learned of sugar from traders from China and India, where it had been produced for centuries. Europeans first tasted sugar in the 12th century, when they crossed the Mediterranean to recover the Holy Land in the Crusades.

## METHODS OF PRODUCTION

The growing and production of crude sugar was back-breaking work. The huge, razor-sharp stalks of sugar cane grew to a height of 12 feet (4m) or taller and were cut and harvested by hand in hot and humid conditions. To prevent it from spoiling, the cane had to be transported within 24 hours to pressing mills, where it was crushed to extract its juice.

The juice was boiled until it became a syrup and was poured into inverted earthenware cones in which it cooled and crystalized. The uncrystalized sugar, called molasses, drained through a hole in the cone, leaving raw, brown unrefined sugar. This was then refined to make it white by dissolving it in water, reboiling it, and recrystallizing the syrup several times. By the 17th century this process was usually carried out in European refineries.

Refining dramatically raised the cost of sugar, and different grades were available from the cheapest coarse raw sugar to the most expensive fine white sugar. Customers could buy an entire cone-shaped loaf, weighing up to 40 lb (18kg) and costing a small fortune, or cut a small amount off a cone.

As the demand for sugar increased, Europeans became eager to grow their own sugar cane. By the 1450s the Portuguese were growing sugar cane on the mid-Atlantic island of Madeira and, by 1490, on the island of São Tomé, off the coast of West Africa. In 1500 they claimed Brazil, where the hot humid climate and abundant water supply were perfect for growing sugar

*Slaves in a pressing mill work at crushing sugar cane to extract the juice. Like many parts of sugar production, this could be a back-breaking task.*

cane. By 1518 the first Brazilian sugar plantation was in operation, and by the 1620s Brazil had become the world's leading sugar producer, with more than 350 sugar plantations.

The Spanish, too, had entered the sugar market at the end of the 15th century, growing sugar on the Canary Islands off the west coast of Africa. In 1493 Christopher Columbus (1451–1506) introduced sugar to the New World on behalf of the Spanish when he brought cane cuttings to the West Indies on his second voyage. The Spanish sugar industry was soon thriving on the islands of Cuba and Hispaniola. From the 1580s onward the English, French, and Dutch also became involved in the sugar industry. At first they participated as sugar refiners and slave importers, but by the mid-1600s they were producing their own sugar on West Indian islands.

## SUGAR CONSUMPTION

As the production of sugar increased and its cost fell, it became a regular part of the European and American diets. This resulted in many very bad teeth. Queen Elizabeth I of England, for example, was so fond of sugary dishes and candies that her teeth went black.

Increased sugar consumption also had a cost in human life. A huge and cheap labor force was required for

the heavy work of growing and harvesting sugar cane, and the expanding sugar industry was one of the biggest contributing factors to the development of the slave trade.

At first European plantation owners employed the native peoples of Brazil and the West Indies, but they soon died out from overwork and European diseases. Slaves imported from Africa became the main source of labor on the plantations. Conditions were terrible. Most slaves were poorly fed and lived in cramped, unhygienic quarters, because it was cheaper to buy new slaves and work them to death than to provide decent living conditions. The result was a massive expansion in the slave trade from around 1650.

*A loaf of sugar is produced by leaving it to crystalize in a cone-shaped container. In the Americas a refining technique known as claying was often used. This involved placing a lump of waterlogged clay over the top of the cones of raw sugar, allowing the water to percolate through and leach out any impurities.*

## SUGAR ART

In the early 16th century people used sugar—which was regarded as a spice—to show off their wealth. Hosts who presented their guests with a table laden with sugary delicacies showed that they were rich enough to afford large quantities of expensive sugar. Cooks created huge, elaborate centerpieces molded from sugar or marchpane, a confection similar to modern marzipan, made from ground almonds, sugar, rosewater, cinnamon, and nutmeg. These sculptures were made in every kind of shape, including castles, boats, and animals, and then intricately decorated with icing made of sugar and rosewater.

SEE ALSO

- Food and drink
- Portugal
- Slave trade
- Spices
- Trade
- West Indies

# SULEYMAN THE MAGNIFICENT

**Sultan Suleyman I (1494 or 1495–1566) ruled the Ottoman Empire from 1520 to 1566. His subjects knew him as Suleyman the Lawgiver. European rulers, dazzled by the splendor of his empire and in awe of his ambition and absolute power, called him Suleyman the Magnificent.**

Suleyman was born in Trabzon on the Black Sea coast of Turkey in 1494 or 1495. His father, Sultan Selim I (ruled 1512–1520), schooled Suleyman to become the perfect ruler.

### SULEYMAN THE LAWGIVER

Many historians regard Suleyman's reign as a model of justice and harmony. Suleyman did not create a system of European-style statute laws. In Islamic tradition the Shariah, or the laws derived from the Koran, are universal and absolute, and cannot be modified or changed by any ruler. Suleyman therefore applied himself to *kanun*, or situational decisions in everyday life not covered by shariah law. In so doing, he elevated *kanun* into an independent code of justice.

Under Suleyman's rule the Ottoman Empire welcomed merchants and refugees of all nationalities and religions. Such toleration prompted the Protestant reformer Martin Luther (1483–1546) to remark that Christians were happier under the Ottomans than under many sovereigns of Europe.

Much of the day-to-day government of the empire was carried out by viziers (chief ministers) and an extensive civil service. Suleyman selected able men to fill administrative posts, and his civil service was organized and efficient. It provided welfare for the poor, and its careful recordkeeping made sure that taxes were collected fairly. It also provided extensive financial support for universities, hospitals, and the arts.

Indeed, Suleyman's reign marked a high point in Ottoman culture, particularly architecture. His building

*This portrait of Suleyman was painted by a 16th-century Venetian artist. Europeans both respected and feared Suleyman.*

projects included new dams and aqueducts, roads, bridges, religious schools, baths, and botanical gardens, both within the capital Istanbul and throughout the empire.

### EXPANDING THE EMPIRE

Suleyman continued the territorial expansion of the Ottoman Empire begun by his predecessors. On the one hand he was at war almost constantly, seeking to extend his empire and to protect and consolidate the lucrative trade routes that ran through his lands. On the other hand he reinforced his power by fostering an atmosphere of tolerance in his empire to attract foreigners and keep his people happy.

Initially Suleyman concentrated his campaigns in central Europe, where he attempted to extend Ottoman rule into Hungary. He destroyed the Hungarian army at the Battle of Mohács in 1526; but his advance further into Europe was halted in 1529, when he failed to capture Vienna in Austria.

Suleyman also focused on winning supremacy in the Mediterranean. He captured the strategically important island of Rhodes, off the southwest coast of present-day Turkey, in 1522. He also enlisted Barbarossa (died 1546), leader of the Barbary pirates, as

commander of the Ottoman fleet. With Barbarossa's help he made territorial gains in North Africa and in 1538 destroyed the combined fleets of Venice, Spain, and the Papal States.

After 1541 Suleyman had to turn east to counter the resurgence of the Persian Empire. He collapsed and died on September 6, 1566, at Szigetvár in southwestern Hungary, while leading his troops on another campaign against the Austrian Hapsburg Empire. He was buried in the specially built Suleymaniye Mosque in Istanbul.

*Suleyman and his army besiege the stronghold of the Knights of Saint John on the Mediterranean island of Rhodes. With a fleet of around 200 ships and an army of nearly 100,000 men Suleyman seized the island in 1522.*

## SULEYMAN'S WIFE

Suleyman broke with the traditions of the Ottoman sultans when he married Roxelane (about 1500–1558), one of his concubines, or mistresses. Roxelane's origin is unknown, but she was probably Russian or Polish. She was captured by Suleyman's forces during an Ottoman military campaign.

After being taken to Istanbul, she became a slave in the sultan's harem, a close and pow-

erful community of advisers, concubines, and family members. She soon became a favorite of Suleyman, and eventually he married her. As the sultan's wife, Roxelane was the most powerful woman in the Ottoman Empire. She plotted to have her sons Bayezid and Selim as Suleyman's successors instead of his older son Mustafa. In this she succeeded, since Selim became sultan on Suleyman's death.

**SEE ALSO**
- Istanbul
- Mohács, Battle of
- Ottoman Empire
- Persian–Ottoman wars
- Pirates and brigands

# SWITZERLAND

**Between 1500 and 1700 Switzerland emerged from the shadows of its powerful neighbors, Burgundy and the Holy Roman Empire, to become a fully independent nation-state. In the Reformation of the 16th century several Swiss cities were major centers of religious debate and reform.**

In 1500 Switzerland was a confederation (league) of eight administrative districts known as cantons. It was greatly strengthened by a series of military victories.

In the 1470s the Swiss towns defeated the Burgundian leader Charles the Bold (ruled 1467–1477). The Swiss then secured their southern borders with a victory over the duke of Milan. Their greatest triumph came in 1499, when, with financial aid from France, they defeated Holy Roman Emperor Maximilian I (ruled 1493–1519). The independence of Switzerland was effectively recognized by Maximilian in the resulting Treaty of Basel (1499); it was formally acknowledged by other nations over a century later under the Treaty of Westphalia (1648).

## VATICAN GUARD
In 1506 Pope Julius II hired Swiss guards to help protect the Vatican in Rome. He chose Swiss soldiers partly because of their reputation as great fighters and partly because of their opposition to Maximilian, who was planning to have himself made pope. Switzerland then went through a brief

*The Swiss reformer Huldrych Zwingli preaches to a congregation in Zurich. Zwingli led the Reformation in Switzerland, and in 1523 Zurich became the first city to accept his reformed religion in place of Roman Catholicism.*

period of expansionism during which it tried to gain control of northern Italy. After its army was defeated by France and Venice at the Battle of Marignano (1515) near Milan, however, the nation adopted a policy of neutrality that still survives. Despite this Switzerland remained a recruiting ground for mercenary armies in the 16th and 17th centuries.

Meanwhile more cantons joined the Swiss confederation. Internal peace was not quickly or easily achieved, however.

### REFORMATION AND CIVIL WAR

Switzerland was a leading center of the Reformation. One of the first wave of reformers was Huldrych Zwingli (1481–1531), a priest in Zurich. He was convinced that Christian faith should be based on the Bible rather than church traditions. He began to institute reforms and by 1525 had won over the city council. He encouraged other Swiss cities to hold public debates on religious reforms. In the ensuing dispute between Switzerland's Catholics and Protestants Zwingli was supported by the cantons of Appenzell, Basel, Bern, Glarus, and Schaffhausen, but opposed by those of Fribourg, Lucerne, Uri, Schwyz, Solothurn, Unterwalden, and Zug. In 1529 civil war broke out; the Protestants were defeated at the Battle of Kappel in 1531, during which Zwingli was killed.

The other Protestant stronghold in the region was Geneva, which at the time was an independent city-state. Geneva had a profound influence on Swiss affairs because John Calvin (1509–1564), its religious and political leader from the late 1530s, sided with the Swiss Protestants, and he intervened decisively on their behalf.

After the Battle of Kappel fighting in Switzerland became sporadic, but enmity between the nation's Catholics

and Protestants continued. The two main flashpoints in Switzerland were the Villmergen wars of 1656 and 1712.

### RELIGIOUS DIVIDE

Much of the conflict was played out in foreign wars in which many Swiss fought as mercenaries. The Catholic cantons supported the Catholic Hapsburgs, while most Swiss Protestant mercenaries fought for France, mainly because that nation was opposed to the Holy Roman Empire (ruled by the Hapsburgs). The division was maintained until 1693, when the alliances switched—Swiss Protestants agreed to fight for the Dutch and English against the French, while the Catholic cantons supplied soldiers for Spain, which allied itself with France against the Austrian Hapsburgs in the War of the Spanish Succession (1701–1714).

*King Francis I of France leads his troops against Swiss soldiers in the Battle of Marignano in September 1515. The Swiss suffered a decisive defeat, loosing 8,000 men, after which they ceased their campaigns to win territories in Italy.*

SEE ALSO
- Calvin, John
- Geneva
- Holy Roman Empire
- Reformation
- Zwingli, Huldrych

# TAXES AND GOVERNMENT FINANCES

During the 1500s and 1600s states needed more and more money to finance both costly military campaigns and their growing governments. To meet these costs, they raised money through a range of different taxes and, increasingly, through loans from wealthy bankers.

Changes in the social and political structure of many European countries from the 14th century onward meant that states needed more revenue (income). As monarchs asserted their authority over nobles and attempted to unify their nations, they came to rely on growing staffs of bureaucrats to administer their governments. They also built up standing (permanent) armies to maintain order and to defend their realms, as well as to wage war on their enemies and expand their territories; previously they had relied on nobles to provide them with troops.

All these developments cost money. Government officials and soldiers had to be paid, and weapons and naval fleets bought. In the 16th and 17th centuries warfare consumed by far the largest share of government spending.

*Peasants line up to pay their taxes in the paper-strewn office of a tax collector in this 17th-century painting by the Flemish artist Pieter Brueghel the Younger (1564–1638).*

Many states struggled to raise enough money to cover the costs of war, which were steadily rising. The price of food rose fivefold between 1500 and 1650, and the cost of manufactured goods tripled, forcing up the cost of feeding and equipping armies. At the same time, wars were being fought between larger and larger armies. Across Europe monarchs increased taxation to try to meet their spiraling expenses.

## EARLY DEVELOPMENTS

In the 14th and 15th centuries the English and French monarchies developed methods of taxation that shaped practices in the following centuries. The impetus behind these developments was the need to raise money for the Hundred Years' War, a long-drawn-out conflict between England and France that dragged on from 1337 to 1453.

In England the monarch called sessions of Parliament to request tax rises rather than imposing them directly and risking the rebellion of nobles or the common people. He or she gave the nobles and city officials more power in return for grants of new taxes. Such taxes usually took the form of a poll, or head, tax, which meant that each household paid based on the number of people living in it.

The English Parliament assumed the right to grant or reject new taxes and to act as an advisory body to the monarch. The House of Commons, which represented the rural gentry and the merchant elites of the city, acquired the right to introduce all tax legislation and to name a committee to examine tax records and supervise tax collection. In this way, by the 16th century England had developed a very reliable system of taxation.

In France during the Hundred Years' War taxation centered on

products consumed by the population, such as salt. The government monopoly on the sale of salt enabled the French crown to raise money by charging a sales tax on this essential commodity. The tax, called the *gabelle*, remained central to the finances of the French government until the French Revolution (1789).

During the final years of the war France also turned to a form of the head tax known as the *taille*. Both taxes fell more heavily on the poor than the rich, because they accounted for a larger proportion of their income. In addition, nobles exempted themselves from many taxes: This was a common problem in many European countries in the 16th and 17th centuries, because monarchs had to bargain with their most powerful subjects to gain their overall support for tax rises.

## IMPORT TAXES AND LOANS

European states in the Reformation era rarely imposed income tax or taxation based on wealth. They far preferred to tax commodities such as salt and flour,

*This painting done by the Flemish artist Pieter Brueghel the Younger in around 1607 shows a census station where villagers had to register their names and the size of their family. This information was then given to government officials in a system that enabled rulers to efficiently tax their subjects.*

# TAX COLLECTION

During the 16th and 17th centuries tax collection played an important part in building centralized and efficient governments. Although rulers in different countries imposed a range of different taxes on their subjects, tax collection was conducted in much the same way everywhere. A government tax collector was sent out to every community to make sure each citizen paid the required tax on their land and produce. Sometimes the imposition of high taxes was followed by rebellions and riots. People involved in these uprisings, like other tax evaders, faced harsh punishments, often including death.

*This 19th-century painting shows Charles V being entertained in the Fugger household. One of the Fuggers burns some bonds, freeing Charles from repaying some of the money he has borrowed from the family.*

or people, as in the head tax. Above all, governments favored taxing goods from abroad. Taxing foreign imports also protected the market for homemade goods—a key idea of mercantilism, the economic approach favored by many countries in Europe at this time. At the same time, it prevented rebellions and riots by the local population. Attempts to impose new taxes frequently led to rebellion across Europe in the period. As the markets grew during the 16th

century, and the volume of trade increased, so did taxes on imports. Merchants across Europe grew wealthy, and governments also tried to get at that wealth. Bankers like the Medici of Florence and the Fuggers of Augsburg loaned money to kings, princes, and even popes, hoping in turn to receive political favor and monetary rewards—in the form of interest payments on the sums loaned, as well as tax exemptions.

## THE FUGGERS

By the 16th century, with Jakob Fugger II (1459–1525) at its head, the Fugger family business had become hugely successful. Jakob moved much of the family's capital (wealth) from trade into mining. He financed mines owned by the Hapsburg duke of Tyrol and later mining enterprises in Hungary.

The Fugger family was so successful that the Spanish King Charles I (ruled 1516–1556), also a member of the Hapsburg Dynasty, turned to them to borrow money in his bid to become the Holy Roman emperor in 1519. Charles borrowed 543,000 gold gulden to bribe the electors, who eventually named him emperor.

Jakob Fugger illustrates the close ties that existed between private financiers and the state: He benefited from numerous favors throughout Charles's reign. The Fuggers loaned Charles large amounts of money in return for a mortgage on crown estates in Spain and a privileged position as one of the Hapsburg's chief financial handlers. Yet while the Hapsburgs made the Fugger family fabulously rich in the 16th century, eventually they also led to their downfall. The Hapsburgs failed to make repayments on loans in 1557, 1575, and 1607. The losses cost the Fuggers their business.

Another important source of state finance during the 16th and 17th

centuries was the influx of silver from the Americas. Spanish conquistadors had found vast natural deposits of silver, as well as smaller supplies of gold, in the territories they conquered in Central and South America. They shipped huge quantities of the precious metals to Europe, where the Spanish crown claimed one-fifth of all the shipments under an import tax known as the *Quinta*, or royal fifth.

Most of the silver passed from Spain to Italy and Germany as the Spanish monarchs used it to pay merchants and soldiers. The state invested little of the silver in economic development or in the long-term stability of the Spanish government. Instead, it was used to pay for expensive wars and quick fixes for the problems of the Hapsburg family as rulers of both Spain and the Holy Roman Empire. The increase in the availability of silver also contributed to inflation, which became a problem across Europe in the late 16th and 17th centuries: With more money in circulation the purchasing power of currency decreased.

## SELLING GOVERNMENT OFFICES

During the 16th and 17th centuries the French government began to raise revenue through the sale of government offices, or jobs. It auctioned off positions in government to buyers who were eager to obtain the social status and tax exemptions—along with the occasional noble title—that were associated with working in the government bureaucracy. The system had the added advantage of creating grateful and loyal bureaucrats, unlike the traditional nobility, who often set themselves in opposition to royal policy to protect their noble privileges.

Later developments in the French government led to more efficient tax collection. Programs initiated by the finance minister Jean-Baptiste Colbert (1619–1683) between 1644 and 1683 largely put an end to inefficient tax collection. Colbert continued the practice of selling offices, including positions such as judge and mayor, and also made guilds pay for the right to enforce trade regulations. He also made sure that the officials collecting taxes returned them to the state, rather than pocketing them or skimming profits off the top.

The pressing need to organize state finances meant that by 1700 many of Europe's governments had brought in important changes. They successfully increased their revenues through a mixture of direct and indirect taxes, loans, and the sale of offices.

*Jean-Baptiste Colbert introduced major reforms that greatly improved French state finances in the 17th century.*

### SEE ALSO

- Banks and banking
- Charles V
- Fugger family
- Government, systems of
- Hapsburg family
- Mercantilism
- Monarchy and absolutism

# TEA AND COFFEE

**Tea was introduced to Europe from China at the beginning of the 17th century, while coffee was brought from West Asia. At first both beverages were drunk only by the wealthy; but as they became cheaper, they became central to European culture.**

Tea has been drunk in China for thousands of years. The Chinese believed that it could cure illnesses and even extend life. It was virtually unknown in Europe until the mid-16th century, when travelers, merchants, and missionaries in Asia began to send back reports of tea drinking to Europe.

Tea is made from the leaves of an evergreen shrub. Once picked, the leaves are dried in different ways, producing either the green tea that was popular in Europe in the 17th century or the black tea that only became popular in the late 18th century.

*Catherine of Braganza, the Portuguese wife of the English King Charles II, was particularly fond of tea. She introduced the custom of serving it at court in translucent, delicate Chinese bowls and pots. Wealthy and fashionable people quickly followed her example.*

### INTRODUCTION OF TEA

Green tea was first introduced to the people of the Netherlands and Portugal in around 1610. By the 1630s tea drinking had reached Germany and France. The Dutch also introduced tea to America in the 1650s. When the English acquired the Dutch colony of New Amsterdam (New York) in 1644, they found that the small settlement consumed more tea at the time than all of England put together.

Tea was first sold in England in 1657. It did not, however, become a popular beverage until 1662, when King Charles II (ruled 1660–1685)

## JAPANESE TEA CEREMONY

In the 12th century the Japanese learned about green tea when a Buddhist monk returned from China and introduced the tea ritual that was practiced in Chinese Zen Buddhist temples. The tea ritual evolved over the centuries into an elegant ceremony, called *Cha-no-yu* ("hot water for tea"), an art form that appeared simple but actually required a great deal of training. At its center was placing powdered green tea in a tea bowl, covering it with hot, not boiling, water, and then beating the mixture into a froth with a tea whisk.

married Catherine of Braganza (1638–1705), a Portuguese princess who loved the drink. Tea did not become a drink of ordinary people until the late 18th century, when it became more affordable.

Prized for its medicinal qualities, tea was initially sold in apothecary shops (the drugstores of the period), along with rare and costly spices that were also believed to have healing properties, such as ginger and nutmeg. By the late 17th century, however, tea was available in food shops and markets.

## THE DRINKING OF COFFEE

During the 16th and 17th centuries coffee beans could only be obtained from the Arabian port of Mocha, at the southern end of the Red Sea in what is now Yemen. The drink called coffee was made by grinding the beans and adding boiling water. It became popular in West Asia in the mid-15th century, when it was adopted as an alternative to alcohol, which is forbidden by Islamic law.

Coffee was introduced into Europe in the early 17th century. In the Mediterranean ports of Venice and Marseilles it was enjoyed by the nobility and the wealthy merchants who imported it. The English were the first Europeans to sell brewed coffee to the public. The first coffeehouse in England was opened in the university town of Oxford in 1650. It was followed by another in London in 1652; by the beginning of the 18th century London had hundreds of coffeehouses of all sizes.

The coffeehouses provided not only coffee but also newspapers for customers to read and tobacco. They were crowded, smelly, noisy, smoky places where artists, intellectuals, merchants, and bankers gathered to discuss politics or do business. Women

were not allowed inside. By the 1680s coffeehouses were thronged everywhere in Europe, and coffee had become so popular that it was replacing beer and wine as the standard morning drink.

In 1690 the Dutch ended the Arabian monopoly on the coffee trade by smuggling a coffee plant out of Mocha and setting up their own coffee plantations in Sri Lanka and Java (in Indonesia). The first Europeans to grow coffee, they were soon followed by others, particularly in the Americas.

*The drinking of coffee, illustrated in this 17th-century engraving, began in Arabia.*

SEE ALSO

- East India companies
- New York
- Spices
- Trade

# TECHNOLOGY

**Technology is the application of knowledge to the practical needs of everyday life. In the 1500s and 1600s Europeans greatly advanced their understanding of the world, and certain technologies, such as printing and firearms—and, later, scientific inventions—became very influential.**

The technology that touched the everyday lives of most Europeans in the 16th and 17th centuries was basic by modern standards, and much of it had already been revived or developed during the Middle Ages. Peasants, who made up more than 80 percent of the European population, continued to use tools and implements, such as plows, carts, scythes, and axes, whose design had evolved centuries earlier.

### BASIC TECHNOLOGY
As before, the main sources of power continued to be humans, draft animals, or waterwheels and windmills. In a period of population growth, when unemployment was high and wages

were low, there was little incentive to create new labor-saving devices either in farming or in the growing number of small industries, such as textile manufacturing, brewing, or tanning (leathermaking). These and other skilled occupations continued to use tools, techniques, and processes that had been handed down by generations of craftsmen.

In regions with plentiful supplies of fast-flowing water waterwheels were used to drive mills that ground grain. They were also used for fulling, a process in clothmaking, and for crushing rock extracted from mines. In flatter regions such as the Netherlands or areas with low rainfall, such as Spain, wind was harnessed to power

*Leonardo da Vinci made these drawings of a scythed chariot and an armored car in about 1487. Both contraptions were intended to breach infantry ranks and were designed for Duke Ludovico Sforza of Milan. They remained unbuilt, like Leonardo's other inventions.*

*This mid–17th-century woodcut shows a printer's workshop. Printing was one of the most influential technologies of the 16th and 17th centuries. Printing businesses sprang up in towns and cities to satisfy the growing demand for reading materials, from Bibles to popular literature.*

such activities. Windmills were also used for drainage, either to draw water out of mine shafts or to reclaim land. In the Netherlands, where much of the land is near or below sea level, windmills were used in combination with dikes, or earth walls, to drain and protect land. In this way the Dutch used existing technology to modify their environment, creating farmland to supply fresh produce to the rapidly growing towns of the Netherlands. The widespread use and refinement of existing technology was typical of the 1500s and 1600s, and characterized activities from building construction, mining, and metalwork to glass and pottery making.

A number of technological advances made in the 1300s and 1400s had a profound effect on European politics, economics, and culture in the following

## THE DEVELOPMENT OF FIREARMS

From 1500 to 1700 great advances were made on the battlefield. Arms, armor, and city defenses were all improved by developments in technology. By the 15th century Europeans knew how to make gunpowder that burned slowly enough for safe use in cannons. Methods of forging and casting metal were also improved. As a result cannons, which were first used to great effect in the Italian Wars (1494–1559), became devastating siege weapons. Medieval castles and city defenses crumbled under cannon attacks. In response rulers employed engineers such as Sébastien le Prestre de Vauban (1633–1707) to devise new defensive plans, which featured low, reinforced walls able to withstand cannon shot and gun placements sited to maximize enemy casualties.

By 1600 firearms had largely replaced traditional weapons such as swords and crossbows in European armies. The earliest firearm that was widely used was the harquebus. It was later developed into the matchlock and flintlock rifles. The matchlock rifle, in which a match or fuse was used to light the gunpowder charge, was replaced in around 1635 by the flintlock rifle, in which a flint struck steel to create a spark.

*A sailing wagon designed by the Flemish inventor Simon Stevin (1548–1620) glides along a beach in this print from 1599. Stevin designed the sailing wagon for Prince Maurice of Nassau. On one occasion the vehicle carried 26 guests on a two-hour trip at an average speed of 25 miles per hour (40km/h).*

centuries. The most influential of these inventions were gunpowder and the development of firearms (*see box p. 59*), improvements in ship design, and the printing press and movable type.

### SHAPING AN AGE

Advances in military and naval technology were often supported by state patronage, since rulers saw advances in both fields as useful ways to extend their power. Developments in firearms led to ever-more devastating weapons and warfare in the 16th and 17th centuries. As rulers fought for domination, they spent huge sums of money on weapons, soldiers, and supplies, and their armies laid waste to urban and rural areas across Europe.

Likewise, the desire of European monarchs to dominate the lucrative spice and commodity trade with Asia spurred advances in ship design. Shipbuilders developed caravels, carracks, galleons, and *fluyts* to satisfy requirements for strong vessels with sufficient sail power to cross oceans and enough space to carry cargoes and armaments. Advances in naval technology—and also in navigation methods and sea charts—enabled explorers to discover oceans and lands previously unknown to Europeans. Combined with military advances, they also enabled traders, conquistadors, and colonists to overpower peoples in regions from Africa and Asia to the Americas, and establish European trading posts and colonies there.

Meanwhile, the printing press and movable metal type revolutionized the way in which information and ideas were disseminated. These inventions made it possible to reproduce texts accurately, quickly, and cheaply—compared to copying by hand—thereby facilitating the spread of new learning and the Protestant religion.

## THE SCIENTIFIC REVOLUTION

Another area of human achievement that came to have a profound influence on technology, particularly from the late 1500s onward, was science. The so-called Scientific Revolution of the 15th, 16th, and 17th centuries was distinguished by a new attitude toward traditionally held ideas about the world. Rather than accepting the theories of ancient Greek and Roman writers, as medieval scholars had done, some thinkers and scientists began to evaluate them more critically. They aimed to discover new theories based on the direct study of the world.

The Italian artist Leonardo da Vinci (1452–1519) was typical of this new spirit of inquiry. He studied the natural world and anatomy, and recorded his observations in many drawings. The knowledge he gained fed his creativity, and he made numerous designs for inventions, from flying machines to submarines and siege machines. Observations of the planets made by the Polish astronomer Nicolaus

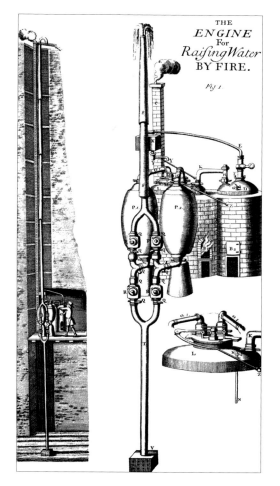

*This 18th-century illustration shows the steam pump designed by the English engineer and inventor Thomas Savery in 1698. Savery's machine, known as the miner's friend, was designed to pump water out of coal mines. It was the first steam engine to be built but was soon superseded by a more practical model designed by another English engineer, Thomas Newcomen, in 1712.*

Copernicus (1473–1543) and his resulting description of a system with the sun at its center signaled a rethinking of long-accepted ideas.

Before the 1500s people had viewed science and technology as two separate pursuits. Craftsmen and artisans built

## SOME FAMILIAR INVENTIONS

A number of technological devices that are familiar today were first invented in the 1500s and 1600s. One example is the flush toilet, which was invented around 1590 by John Harington (1561–1612), a godson of Queen Elizabeth I of England. Harington invented a valve that, when pulled, would release a water holder to flush away the contents of the toilet. The submarine is another apparently modern invention that actually dates from the Renaissance. Leonardo da Vinci produced designs for submarines, although they remained unbuilt. Around a century later, in 1620, the Dutch engineer Cornelis Drebbel (1572–1633) constructed a submarine for the English navy. It was made from wood covered with greased leather and was propelled by oars fitted through watertight seals. Tubes attached to the hull carried air from the surface inside the submarine to the mariner.

*The Frenchman Florin Périer uses a barometer to measure air pressure on the Puy-de-Dome Mountain in France around 1648. He undertook the experiment for his brother-in-law, the scientist and philosopher Blaise Pascal, who wanted to prove that air pressure dropped with altitude.*

and designed tools and other devices, while scientists, who were known as natural philosophers, speculated on the properties of the world by pure thought. However, from the late 1500s thinkers such as the Italian Galileo Galilei (1564–1642), the Englishman Robert Boyle (1627–1691), and the Frenchman Blaise Pascal (1623–1662) pioneered a new method of looking at the world using instruments.

## SCIENCE AND TECHNOLOGY

Technology assisted the progress of scientific understanding through the creation of accurate instruments such as microscopes, telescopes, and accurate measuring devices such as rulers and clocks. Meanwhile, scientific discoveries led to advances in technology through the understanding that they brought of natural laws. For example, the investigations into pendulum motion by the Dutchman Christiaan Huygens (1629–1695) enabled him to build the most accurate clock of the age.

Several areas of science led to new technology. Some of the greatest scientific achievements in the 16th and 17th centuries were made by the English physicist Isaac Newton (1642–1727), in particular his work on light and gravity. Knowledge of optics assisted lensmakers in shaping glass lenses to magnify objects or correct poor eyesight and ultimately led to the invention of the compound microscope in 1595 and the telescope in 1608.

Another area of science that proved central to technology was the physics of gases, investigated by Robert Boyle. His findings led the Italian scientists Evangelista Torricelli (1608–1647) and Vincenzo Viviani (1622–1703) to invent an accurate barometer in 1643. More importantly, knowledge about gases led to the use of steam as a source of power. The French physicist Denis Papin (1647–about 1712) and the English engineers Thomas Savery (about 1650–1715) and Thomas Newcomen (1663–1729) pioneered steam technology. In 1712 Newcomen built the first practical steam engine, an invention that was of huge importance to the later Industrial Revolution.

**SEE ALSO**
- Astronomy
- Clocks and calendars
- Guilds and crafts
- Inventions and inventors
- Mining
- Printing
- Science
- Ships
- Warfare

# TERESA OF AVILA

**The Spanish nun Teresa of Avila (1515–1582) was one of the great
figures of the Roman Catholic church; she was made a saint in 1622.
She is known for her extreme piety and intense religious visions; she
introduced far-reaching reforms to the Carmelite order.**

Teresa was the daughter of a rich
merchant and grew up in the
town of Avila in central Spain.
She decided to become a nun against
the wishes of her father and in 1535
ran away to join the local Carmelite
convent. In 1536 Teresa became
seriously ill and did not fully recover
until 1539. She attributed her return
to health to the prayers she had made
to Saint Joseph.

## VISIONS AND MYSTICISM

During the following years Teresa led
an uneventful life in her convent. Then,
in about 1554, she was praying in front
of a small statue of Christ when she
felt a deep spiritual warmth inside her
—an experience she later thought of as
a "second conversion" to the Christian
faith. From this time she experienced
a growing number of visions and
locutions (divine voices).

Some of Teresa's colleagues became
alarmed at these phenomena, believing
them to be inspired by the Devil.
Teresa, however, firmly believed that
they came from God. She interpreted
them as mystical events in which she
experienced the divine through her
senses. She was supported in her view
by a number of followers, including the
Franciscan mystic and reformer Saint
Peter of Alcantara (1499–1562).
Teresa's mystical experiences came
to a climax in 1559 when she fell
into a state of ecstasy and felt an

angel pierce her heart with a flaming
spear, or dart, an event later called the
"transverberation."

## REFORMING THE CARMELITES

In her later years Teresa concentrated
on reforming the Carmelite Order. She
considered that the atmosphere in her

*In this 17th-
century painting
celebrating the
Carmelite Order,
Teresa (right) holds
an arrow to her
heart, as a symbol
of her vision.*

convent was too relaxed. Teresa wanted a stricter, more disciplined religious life. On August 24, 1562, she established in Avila a new convent of Carmelites. They were known as the Discalced (shoeless or barefoot) Carmelites because their piety extended to wearing only sandals or going barefoot.

Teresa's actions displeased some members of the order but impressed its head. He permitted Teresa to found more religious houses. With her friend and fellow mystic John of the Cross (1542–1591) she founded a monastery in Duruelo in 1568. She also set up religious houses at Toledo (1569), Salamanca (1570), and Segovia (1574).

During the 1570s Teresa began to write her *Book of Foundations* (1610), in which she relates the establishment of the new convents. In 1577, after another vision, she began her greatest work, *The Interior Castle* (1588), a symbolic account of the soul's journey toward God.

### ROYAL SUPPORT

Although the discalced foundations helped reinvigorate the religious life of Spain, some members of the Spanish church objected to the changes Teresa was making. In 1580 the disputes were brought to an end when the Spanish King Philip II (ruled 1556–1598) gave the order his support. By this time Teresa's health was declining. She founded three more convents, at Palencia, Soria, and Burgos, before she died in October 1582.

*Saint Teresa talks to Christ in this illustration of one of her visions. Teresa believed that her mystical experiences brought her into direct union with the divine.*

# TERESA'S WRITINGS

The Counter Reformation placed new emphasis on personal spiritual experiences gained by way of the senses. The visions of Teresa of Avila combined sensory experience and religious contemplation. Teresa's activities resulted in a significant literary expression. A prolific writer, she was one of the first women in Spain to publish her works. By exploring the divine fulfillment in written accounts of her visions, Teresa profoundly influenced religious verse in the late 16th century and 17th century. Two writers particularly influenced by her were John of the Cross, a close friend with whom she worked, and the English Catholic poet Richard Crashaw (1613–1649). Teresa is recognized as one of the most colorful personalities to participate in shaping a new language of mysticism.

SEE ALSO
- Council of Trent
- Counter Reformation
- Jesuits
- Papacy
- Sculpture

# TEXTILES

The production of textiles was established as an important part of many European economies by the 11th century. From that time until the 19th century the industry in northern countries depended heavily on wool and linen, while in Italy the emphasis was on the production of silks.

From 1500 most people wore clothes made of wool. Largely carried out in people's homes, the various processes involved in the production of woolen cloth supported many northern European communities in 1500. They were responsible for Flanders (in present-day Belgium) being one of the richest, most densely populated regions in Europe. Both there and in France were towns where wool was woven into cloth and tapestries. Linen production became more popular in the 17th century.

## TAPESTRY PRODUCTION

Tapestries were woven from threads of fine wool and sometimes gold and silver. They were hung on the walls of the castles and houses of the wealthy to provide insulation from the cold, damp climate of northern Europe. They were also status symbols, being extremely expensive because of the materials from which they were woven and the time and skill required to make them. It could take a team of skilled weavers over a year to produce a single tapestry.

Rulers cherished the propaganda value of tapestries, which could be woven with designs to glorify their achievements. For example, the Holy Roman Emperor Charles V (ruled 1519–1556) ordered tapestries to commemorate his major battle victories, such as *The Battle of Pavia* woven around 1530. Such tapestries

were regarded as works of art and the equal of any painting. Many leading painters, such as Rubens (1577–1640), also designed tapestries.

## TURKISH RUGS

Carpets made in Anatolia (Turkey) were another highly prized furnishing in wealthy European homes. European merchants imported them in significant

*Eleanor, wife of the Florentine Duke Cosimo de' Medici, is portrayed with one of her sons. Her dress is a superb example of the finest textiles of the 16th century.*

## INDIAN COTTONS

In 1600 the English East India Company was set up to develop trade in Southeast Asia and India. It was followed by the creation of the Dutch East India Company in 1602 and a similar French company in 1664. European merchants soon realized that they could make profits not only from the spices of the region but also from its brightly colored textiles—both embroideries and painted cottons.

Cotton fabric painted with designs had been produced in India since ancient times and was used for bedspreads, wall hangings, floor coverings, and clothes, as well as for export to Persia and Southeast Asia. There was an enormous variety of designs, but many featured plants, flowers, and hunting scenes. Even the newly arrived European merchants were sometimes depicted. Europeans soon began to export Indian textiles, both as part of their trade with Southeast Asia and back to their home countries. In Europe by the second half of the 17th century Indian cottons had become popular for furnishings, such as bed covers and curtains for four-poster beds, and for informal clothing, such as dressing gowns and morning gowns.

numbers in the 15th century, and in the 16th and 17th centuries Turkish carpet production increased hugely, with many rugs being made expressly for export. The carpets were woven from wool and had stylized, often geometric designs in rich reds, vivid yellows, blues, and greens. Far too precious to use as floor coverings, they were displayed on table tops or hung on walls.

### SILK PRODUCTION

While tapestry making was the most prestigious form of textile production in northern Europe, the manufacture of silk fabrics dominated Italian output. By 1500 a number of Italian cities were firmly established as centers of silk making. The fabrics produced ranged from plain woven silks to elaborately patterned and textured materials, such as velvets, damasks, lampas, and brocades. Many also featured glittering gold and silver threads.

The heaviest of these silks— velvets and brocades—were used for furnishings, such as curtains, bed covers, and upholstery, as well as for the clothing of the richest members of society. Lighter silks were used for

*The skills of tapestry makers are illustrated in this engraving of 1555. In the 16th century tapestries began to feature realistic figures and spatial effects, rather than the traditional mass of detailed decoration.*

clothes and wall coverings. All these fabrics typically had designs based on plant forms, such as pomegranates, pineapples, pine cones, thistles, leaves, and flowers. Silk thread was also made into sumptuous embroideries that were used to decorate clothes and interiors.

Other highly valued textiles in the 16th and 17th centuries included fine, patterned linen damasks, which were a speciality of the Netherlands. They were used in particular to make sets of tablecloths and napkins. Lace made from linen thread was another Dutch speciality, and it was displayed in large lace collars and cuffs. Venice, Genoa, and Lyons were also important centers for lace making

## FRENCH DOMINANCE

Political events often influenced textile production. The religious persecution and civil war that beset the Netherlands in the second half of the 16th century led many Flemish weavers to flee the region. Elsewhere royal patronage (support) had an effect. King Henry IV of France (ruled 1589–1610) established a tapestry industry in Paris in 1607, and King James I of England (ruled 1603–1625) set up a manufacturing center in London. Both were staffed by Flemish weavers.

The most influential patronage of the 16th and 17th centuries came from King Louis XIV of France. He favored French textiles over fabrics imported from abroad and in 1662 established the Gobelins factory in Paris to provide him with the very best decorative arts for his royal palaces. With strong government support French textile makers came to dominate the production of high-quality tapestries and silks at the end of the 17th century.

Protection of national wool and silk industries also led the governments of France and England to pass laws—in

1686 and 1700 respectively—to ban the import of a new type of textile that seemed ready to rival established industries. Earlier in the 17th century the East India trading companies of the Netherlands, England, and France had begun to import cottons decorated with bright, exotic designs from India (*see box p. 66*). These fabrics had proved a commercial success, and in the second half of the 17th century some European manufacturers began to produce similar designs that they printed using wooden blocks.

The French and English governments banned the import and production of such textiles. However, printed cottons later came to dominate the European textile industry, particularly in the 19th century during the Industrial Revolution.

*Young French girls learn to spin yarn from raw wool in this 17th-century picture. The yarn would subsequently be dyed and woven into cloth, which was then cleaned and stretched.*

SEE ALSO

- Decorative arts
- Dress
- East India companies
- Guilds and crafts
- India
- Manufacturing
- Privacy and luxury

# TIMELINE

♦ **1492** Christopher Columbus lands in the Bahamas, claiming the territory for Spain.

♦ **1494** Charles VIII of France invades Italy, beginning four decades of Italian wars.

♦ **1494** The Treaty of Tordesillas divides the "new world" between Spain and Portugal.

♦ **1498** Portuguese navigator Vasco da Gama sails around Africa to reach Calicut, India.

♦ **1509** Dutch humanist scholar Desiderius Erasmus publishes *In Praise of Folly*, a satire on religion and society.

♦ **1511** The Portuguese capture Melaka in Southeast Asia.

♦ **1515** Francis I of France invades Italy, capturing Milan.

♦ **1516** Charles, grandson of Holy Roman emperor Maximilian I, inherits the Spanish throne as Charles I.

♦ **1517** The German monk Martin Luther nails his Ninety-five Theses to a church door in Wittenberg, Germany, setting the Reformation in motion.

♦ **1518** The Portuguese begin trading in slaves from Africa.

♦ **1519** Charles I of Spain is elected Holy Roman emperor as Charles V.

♦ **1519–1521** Spanish conquistador Hernán Cortés conquers Mexico for Spain.

♦ **1520** Suleyman the Magnificent becomes sultan of the Ottoman Empire.

♦ **1520** Portuguese navigator Ferdinand Magellan rounds the tip of South America and is the first European to sight the Pacific Ocean.

♦ **1521** Pope Leo X excommunicates Martin Luther.

♦ **1521** At the Diet of Worms, Luther refuses to recant his views. The Holy Roman emperor outlaws him.

♦ **1522** One of Magellan's ships completes the first circumnavigation of the globe.

♦ **1523** Gustav Vasa becomes king of Sweden and dissolves the Kalmar Union that had dominated Scandinavia.

♦ **1523–1525** Huldrych Zwingli sets up a reformed church in Zurich, Switzerland.

♦ **1525** Holy Roman Emperor Charles V defeats and captures Francis I of France at the Battle of Pavia.

♦ **1525** In Germany the Peasants' Revolt is crushed; its leaders, including the radical Thomas Münzer, are executed.

♦ **1525** William Tyndale translates the New Testament into English.

♦ **1526** Mongol leader Babur invades northern India and establishes the Mogul Empire.

♦ **1526** At the Diet of Speyer German princes are granted the authority to allow Lutheran teachings and worship in their own territories.

♦ **1526** Suleyman the Magnificent defeats Hungarian forces at the Battle of Mohács.

♦ **1527** Charles V's forces overrun Italy and sack Rome.

♦ **1529** In the Peace of Cambrai with Charles V, Francis I of France renounces all French claims in Italy temporarily confirming Spanish supremacy.

♦ **1529** The Ottoman sultan Suleyman the Magnificent besieges the city of Vienna.

♦ **1531** German Protestant princes form the Schmalkaldic League to defend themselves.

♦ **1531–1532** Spanish conquistador Francisco Pizarro conquers Peru for Spain by defeating the Inca Empire.

♦ **1532** Niccolò Machiavelli's *The Prince* is published.

♦ **1534** The earl of Kildare, Thomas Lord Offaly, leads a revolt against Henry VIII's rule in Ireland.

♦ **1534** Henry VIII of England breaks away from the authority of the pope and establishes the Church of England.

♦ **1534** Martin Luther publishes his German translation of the New Testament.

♦ **1535–1536** The city of Geneva adopts Protestantism and expels all Catholic clergy.

♦ **1536** Henry VIII orders the dissolution of the monasteries.

♦ **1536** John Calvin publishes his *Institutes of the Christian Religion*, which sets out central Protestant principles.

♦ **1539** Ignatius Loyola founds the Society of Jesus (Jesuits).

♦ **1541** John Calvin sets up a model Christian community in Geneva, Switzerland.

♦ **1542** Pope Paul III reestablishes the Inquisition, a medieval religious court designed to combat heresy.

♦ **1543** The Flemish anatomist Andreas Vesalius publishes his handbook of anatomy *On the Structure of the Human Body*.

♦ **1543** Polish astronomer Nicolaus Copernicus publishes *On the Revolutions of the Heavenly Orbs*, which challenged contemporary beliefs by describing a sun-centered universe.

♦ **1545** Pope Paul III organizes the Council of Trent to counter the threat of Protestantism and reinvigorate the church.

♦ **1547** Ivan IV (the Terrible) becomes czar of Russia.

♦ **1547** Charles V defeats the Schmalkaldic League at the Battle of Mühlberg.

♦ **1553** Mary I restores the Catholic church in England.

♦ **1555** In the Peace of Augsburg Charles V allows German princes to decide the religion in their territories.

♦ **1555** Charles V abdicates, dividing his vast lands between his brother Ferdinand and son Philip.

♦ **1558** On the death of Mary I, her half-sister Elizabeth I becomes queen of England.

♦ **1559** Elizabeth I restores the Church of England.

♦ **1559** Pope Paul IV institutes the Index of Prohibited Books.

♦ **1562** The Wars of Religion break out in France.

♦ **1563** The Council of Trent ends having clarified Catholic doctrine and laid the basis of the Counter Reformation.

♦ **1566** The Dutch begin a revolt against Spanish rule.

♦ **1569** Flemish cartographer Gerardus Mercator publishes a world map using a new method of projection.

♦ **1571** Philip II of Spain leads an allied European force to victory over the Ottomans at the naval Battle of Lepanto.

♦ **1572** French Catholics murder thousands of Protestants across France in the Saint Bartholomew's Day Massacre.

♦ **1579** Seven Dutch provinces form the Union of Utrecht to fight for independence from Spanish rule.

♦ **1582** The warlord Toyotomi Hideyoshi becomes effective ruler of Japan.

♦ **1588** Philip II launches the Armada invasion fleet against England, but it is destroyed.

♦ **1590** Toyotomi Hideyoshi expels Christian missionaries from Japan.

♦ **1593** The English playwright William Shakespeare publishes his first work, *Venus and Adonis* beginning his prolific and successful career in the theater.

♦ **1598** The Persian Safavid ruler Shah Abbas the Great moves his capital to Esfahan.

♦ **1598** In the Edict of Nantes Henry IV of France grants Huguenots considerable rights, bringing an end to the French Wars of Religion.

♦ **1600** The English East India Company is founded in London to control trade with India and East Asia.

♦ **1602** The Dutch government establishes the Dutch East India Company.

♦ **1603** In Japan Tokugawa Ieyasu unites the country under his rule as shogun, ushering in a age of peace and prosperity.

♦ **1603** James VI of Scotland also becomes king of England as James I on the death of Elizabeth I.

♦ **1605** The Gunpowder Plot: A group of Catholics including Guy Fawkes fail to blow up the English Parliament.

♦ **1607** Henry Hudson sails to the Barents Sea in search of a northeastern passage to Asia.

♦ **1607** John Smith founds the English colony of Jamestown in Virginia.

♦ **1611** James I's authorized Bible, the King James Version, is published.

♦ **1616** Cardinal Richelieu becomes the prime minister of France.

♦ **1618** The Defenestration of Prague marks the beginning of the Thirty Years' War.

♦ **1620** The *Mayflower* pilgrims found the colony of New Plymouth in Massachusetts.

♦ **1621** Huguenots (French Protestants) rebel against King Louis XIII of France.

♦ **1625** Charles I is crowned king of England.

♦ **1629** Charles I dissolves Parliament and rules independently until 1640.

♦ **1631** The Mogul Emperor Shah Jahan builds the Taj Mahal as a mausoleum for his wife Mumtaz.

♦ **1632** Galileo Galilei publishes his *Dialogue Concerning the Two Chief World Systems,* in which he supports Copernicus's views of a sun-centered universe.

♦ **1633** Galileo is tried for heresy and sentenced to house arrest by the Roman Inquisition.

♦ **1637–1638** After a rebellion led by Christians in Japan 37,000 Japanese Christians are executed and many Europeans expelled from the country.

♦ **1640** Portuguese peasants rebel against Spanish rule and declare John of Braganza their king. Portugal finally regains its independence in 1668.

♦ **1641** French philosopher René Descartes publishes one of his most important works, *Meditations on First Philosophy.*

♦ **1642** Civil war breaks out in England between the king and Parliament.

♦ **1642** Jules Mazarin follows Cardinal Richelieu to become prime minister of France.

♦ **1643** Louis XIV becomes king of France. During his reign France becomes powerful.

♦ **1648** The Thirty Years' War comes to an end with the Treaty of Westphalia.

♦ **1648–1653** The Fronde, a series of civil wars, breaks out in France.

♦ **1649** The English king Charles I is executed and England becomes a republic.

♦ **1652** England and the Dutch Republic clash in the first Anglo-Dutch Naval War.

♦ **1653** The English Puritan Oliver Cromwell dissolves Parliament and rules England as lord protector.

♦ **1660** The English Parliament restores Charles II as king.

♦ **1660** The Royal Society of London is founded to promote scientific enquiry.

♦ **1661** Louis XIV begins work on the palace of Versailles outside Paris.

♦ **1661** Manchu Emperor Kang-hsi comes to power in China. His long reign marks a golden age in Chinese history.

♦ **1665** The Great Plague in London kills around a thousand people every week.

♦ **1666** French minister Jean-Baptiste Colbert establishes the French Academy to promote the sciences.

♦ **1666** The Great Fire of London destroys a large part of the English capital.

♦ **1670** The English Hudson's Bay Company is founded to occupy lands and trade in North America.

♦ **1678** English Puritan writer John Bunyan publishes his hugely popular allegorical book *Pilgrim's Progress.*

♦ **1683** The Turkish Ottoman army besieges Vienna for the second time.

♦ **1685** Louis XIV revokes the Edict of Nantes, depriving French Protestants of all religious and civil liberties. Hundreds of thousands of Huguenots flee France.

♦ **1688** In the Glorious Revolution the Protestant Dutch leader, William of Orange, is invited to replace James II as king of England.

♦ **1689** The Bill of Rights establishes a constitutional monarchy in England. William III and his wife Mary II jointly rule England and Scotland.

♦ **1694** The Bank of England is founded in London.

♦ **1699** Turks withdraw from Austria and Hungary.

♦ **1700–1721** The Great Northern War between Sweden and Russia and its allies weakens Swedish power.

♦ **1701** The War of the Spanish Succession breaks out over the vacant Spanish throne.

♦ **1704** Isaac Newton publishes his book *Optics* on the theory of light and color.

♦ **1707** The Act of Union unites England and Scotland. The seat of Scottish government is moved to London.

♦ **1712** Peter the Great makes Saint Petersburg the new capital of Russia, beginning a period of westernization.

♦ **1713–1714** The treaties of Utrecht are signed by England and France, ending the War of the Spanish Succession.

♦ **1715** The sun king King Louis XIV of France dies, marking the end of a golden age in French culture.

# GLOSSARY

**Absolutism**
A system of government in which far-reaching power is held by a monarch or ruler over his or her subjects.

**Alchemy**
A tradition of investigative thought that tried to explain the relationship between humanity and the universe and exploit it, for example, by finding a way to turn base metal into gold.

**Baroque**
An artistic style originating in the 17th century characterized by dramatic effects and ornamentation, which aimed to evoke a strong emotional response.

**Calvinists**
Followers of the French Protestant reformer John Calvin. Calvinism emphasized the sovereignty of God and predestination—the idea that that God decided in advance who would gain eternal life.

**Counter Reformation**
The Catholic church's efforts to reinvigorate itself, bring an end to abuses, clarify its teachings, and prevent the spread of Protestantism.

**Diet**
An assembly of the rulers of the Holy Roman Empire, who gathered to pass laws and make important decisions.

**Doctrine**
A specific principle or belief, or system of beliefs, taught by a religious faith.

**Elector**
A leading landowner in the Holy Roman Empire who had a vote in the election of the Holy Roman emperor.

**Enclosure**
A process by which major landowners extended their holdings across common land.

**Excommunication**
A punishment in which a person was banned from taking part in the rites of the Catholic church.

**Franciscans**
Members of a Catholic religious order founded in the early 13th century by Saint Francis of Assisi.

**Guild**
An association of merchants, professionals, or craftsmen organized to protect the interests of its members and to regulate the quality and cost of their services.

**Heresy**
A belief that is contrary to the teachings of a religious faith.

**Huguenots**
The name given to Calvinists in France.

**Humanism**
An academic approach based on the study of "humanities"—that is, ancient Greek and Roman texts, history, and philosophy—which stressed the importance of developing rounded, cultured individuals.

**Iconoclasm**
The destruction of religious objects, usually by those who disapproved of the use of images in worship.

**Indulgences**
The cancelation or reduction of punishments for sins granted by the Catholic church in return for good works or money.

**Inquisition**
A powerful medieval religious court that was revived by the Catholic church in the 16th century to stamp out ideas contrary to Catholic teachings.

**Janissaries**
Members of an elite infantry corps in the Ottoman army.

**Jesuits**
Members of a Catholic order founded in the 16th century by Ignatius Loyola. They were famous for their work as educators and missionaries.

**Laity or laypeople**
Members of a religious faith who are not clergy.

**Lutherans**
Followers of the German Protestant reformer Martin Luther. He protested against abuses in the Catholic church and argued that the scriptures, not church traditions, were the ultimate religious authority.

**Mass or Eucharist**
A key Christian sacrament of thanksgiving for the sacrifice of Jesus's life celebrated with wine and bread representing his body and blood.

**Mercantilism**
An economic system under which a government regulated manufacturing and trade in the belief that high exports and low imports would enrich the country's treasury and make the state powerful.

**Mercenary**
A soldier who fights for any employer in return for wages.

**Papacy**
The pope and his advisers in Rome who govern the Catholic church.

**Patriarch**
The title given to Orthodox church leaders: The most important patriarchs were the bishops of Antioch, Rome, Alexandria, Constantinople, and Jerusalem.

**Patron**
Someone who orders and pays for a work of art or supports, usually financially, the work of an artist or thinker.

**Protestant**
Someone who follows one of the Christian churches set up during the Reformation in reaction to the corruption of the Catholic church.

**Sacrament**
An important Christian ritual, or ceremony, such as Mass or baptism. The number and nature of the sacraments were issues of major debate during the Reformation.

**Secular**
A term to describe something nonreligious as opposed to something religious.

**Theology**
The study of religion.

**Tithe**
A tax of one-tenth of a person's annual produce or income payable to the church.

**Usury**
The practice of making a dishonest profit, such as charging high interest on a loan, which was considered sinful by the medieval church.

**Vernacular**
The everyday language spoken by the people of a country or region, rather than a literary or formal language such as Latin.

# FURTHER READING

Barry, J., M. Hester, and G. Roberts (eds.). *Witchcraft in Early Modern Europe: Studies in Culture and Belief.* New York: Cambridge University Press, 1996.

Black, C. F. *Church, Religion, and Society in Early Modern Italy.* New York: Palgrave, 2001.

Boorstin, Daniel J. *The Discoverers.* New York: Harry N. Abrams, 1991.

Collinson, Patrick. *The Reformation: A History.* New York: Modern Library, 2004.

Darby, G. (ed.). *The Origins and Development of the Dutch Revolt.* New York: Routledge, 2001.

Dixon, C. S. *The Reformation in Germany.* Malden, Mass.: Blackwell Publishers, 2002.

Duffy, Eamon. *Saints and Sinners: A History of the Popes.* New Haven, Conn.: Yale University Press, 1997.

Elliott , J. H. *Europe Divided 1559–1598.* Second edition, Malden, Mass.: Blackwell Publishers, 2000.

Gäbler, U., and R.C.L. Gritsch (trans.). *Huldrych Zwingli: His Life and Work.* Philadelphia: Fortress Press, 1998.

Goodwin, Jason. *Lords of the Horizons: A History of the Ottoman Empire.* New York: Henry Holt, 1999.

Henry, J. *The Scientific Revolution and the Origins of Modern Science.* Second edition, New York: Palgrave, 2001.

Jaffer, Amin, and Anna Jackson (eds.). *Encounters: The Meeting of Asia and Europe 1500–1800.* New York: Harry N. Abrams, 2004.

Jewell, Helen M. *Education in Early Modern England.* New York: St. Martin's Press, 1998.

Jones, M. D. W. *The Counter Reformation: Religion and Society in Early Modern Europe.* New York: Cambridge University Press, 1995.

Klein, Herbert S. *The Atlantic Slave Trade.* New York: Cambridge University Press, 1999.

Kuhn, Thomas S. *The Copernican Revolution.* New York: MJF Books, 1997.

Lane, Kris. *Pillaging the Empire: Piracy in the Americas, 1500–1750.* Armok, NY: M. E. Sharpe, 1998.

Lindberg, Carter (ed.). *The European Reformation Sourcebook.* Malden, Mass.: Blackwell Publishers, 1999.

MacCulloch, Diarmaid. *The Reformation: A History.* New York: Viking Press, 2004.

Marius, R. *Martin Luther: The Christian between God and Death.* Cambridge, Mass.: Belknap Press, 1999.

McGrath, A. E. *Reformation Thought.* Third edition, Malden, Mass.: Blackwell Publishers, 1999.

Oakley, S. P. *War and Peace in the Baltic 1560–1790.* New York: Routledge, 1992.

Porter, Roy. *The Greatest Benefit to Mankind: Medical History of Humanity.* New York: W. W. Norton, 1998.

Rawlings, Helen. *The Spanish Inquisition.* Malden, Mass.: Blackwell Publishers, 2005.

*Renaissance.* Danbury, Connecticut: Grolier, 2002.

Roth, Mitchel P. *Crime and Punishment: A History of the Criminal Justice System.* Belmont, CA: Thomson Wadsworth, 2005.

Russell-Wood, A. J. R. *The Portuguese Empire, 1415–1808: A World on the Move.* Baltimore, MD: Johns Hopkins University Press, 1998.

Schama, Simon. *The Embarrassment of Riches: Dutch Culture in the Golden Age.* New York: Vintage Books, 1997.

Stoyle, John. *Europe Unfolding 1648–1688.* Second edition, Malden, Mass.: Blackwell Publishers, 2000.

Taylor, Alan. *American Colonies: The Settlement of North America to 1800.* New York: Penguin Books, 2003.

Tracy, J. D. *Europe's Reformations 1450–1650.* Lanham: Rowman & Littlefield, 1999.

Walvin, James. *The Quakers: Money and Morals.* London: John Murray, 1997.

Ware, Timothy. *The Orthodox Church.* New York: Penguin Books, 2004.

Wilson, P. H. *The Holy Roman Empire, 1495–1806.* New York: St. Martin's Press, 1999.

## WEBSITES

*BBC Online: History*
www.bbc.co.uk/history

*British Civil Wars, Commonwealth, and Protectorate 1638–1660*
www.british-civil-wars.co.uk

*Catholic Encyclopedia*
www.newadvent.org/cathen/

*Database of Reformation Artists*
www.artcyclopedia.com/index.html

*History of Protestantism*
www.doctrine.org/history/

*The Library of Economics and Liberty*
www.econlib.org

*National Gallery of Art*
www.nga.gov

*National Maritime Museum, Greenwich*
www.nmm.ac.uk

*Reformation History*
www.historychannel.com

# SET INDEX

Volume numbers are in **bold**.
Page numbers in *italics* refer to
pictures or their captions.

# PICTURE CREDITS